FISHERMAN
RESOURCES

RECKLESS

LIVING PASSIONATELY
AS IMPERFECT CHRISTIANS

FAITH

JO KADLECEK

SHAW BOOKS
an imprint of WATERBROOK PRESS

Reckless Faith
A SHAW BOOK
PUBLISHED BY WATERBROOK PRESS
12265 Oracle Boulevard, Suite 200
Colorado Springs, Colorado 80921
A division of Random House, Inc.

All Scripture quotations, unless otherwise indicated, are taken from the *Holy Bible, New International Version*®. NIV®. Copyright © 1973, 1978, 1984 by International Bible Society. Used by permission of Zondervan Publishing House. All rights reserved.

ISBN 978-0-87788-089-9

Copyright © 2003 by Jo Kadlecek

All rights reserved. No part of this book may be reproduced or transmitted in any form or by any means, electronic or mechanical, including photocopying and recording, or by any information storage and retrieval system, without permission in writing from the publisher.

SHAW BOOKS and its aspen leaf logo are trademarks of WaterBrook Press, a division of Random House, Inc.

Printed in the United States of America
2007

10 9 8 7 6 5 4 3

CONTENTS

MEETING PETER

"It doesn't happen all at once," said the Skin Horse. "You become. It takes a long time. That's why it doesn't often happen to people who break easily, or have sharp edges, or who have to be carefully kept. Generally by the time you are Real, most of your hair has been loved off, and your eyes drop out and you get loose in the joints and very shabby. But these things don't matter at all, because once you are Real you can't be ugly, except to people who don't understand."

—MARGERY WILLIAMS, *The Velveteen Rabbit*

I've always been drawn to authentic people. You know the type: sincere, honest, unpretentious. Okay, so her hair is a little messed up or his kitchen sink has dirty dishes in it. Somehow, these things don't matter because you feel relaxed in his presence, unhurried and free to be yourself because she's relaxed and free as well. In fact, there's nothing slick or showy in her actions. He might even cry when he sees something sappy or sentimental, and, frankly, he doesn't care who might see him.

Yes, these are the people we'd trust with our secrets or confess our fears to. Why? Because they've shown us theirs; they have dared to be real with us. And in a culture where the pressure to compare ourselves to others is great, that is no small thing. Naturally, then, we are drawn to these unique individuals who somehow have discovered the marvelous gift of knowing what it means to be themselves.

This is the reason I have always loved the apostle Peter. If ever there was an example in biblical literature of an authentic individual, a man replete with inconsistencies, emotional extremes, and human frailties, it was Peter. He was impulsive and passionate, cowardly and contradictory. He was intimate with the most Self-less Individual who ever walked the planet, and yet Peter remained immensely self-absorbed. He was presumptuous and argumentative, yet loyal and tender-hearted. He was sometimes thoughtless, fickle, and dishonest, though he was certainly hard working and devoted. And because of all these attributes, Peter is perhaps one of the most complex and interesting characters in all of literature. Peter knew the tension of being fully alive.

But Peter also knew what it meant to be utterly humiliated. Not only did he fall short time and again in his efforts to please his Friend and King, Scripture holds little back in painting a picture of Peter's many foibles, publicly exposing the apostle's mess-ups. What's more astounding to me, however, is the likelihood that after Christ's death and resurrection and before the Gospels were written, Peter actually included many of these humiliating details in his preaching. In short, he *boasted* of his weaknesses.

Peter's traveling companion, Mark, obviously listened well since, in the gospel according to Mark, he included those same stories of Peter's arrogance, shortcomings, and especially, his denial of the Lord. Likewise, in their accounts of Jesus' life, Matthew, Luke, and John aired some of Peter's dirty laundry, revealing more of his quirks and breakdowns. Thanks to their combined reporting, Peter may be the most famous person in all of history who is known more for his failures than for his accomplishments. People joke about Peter. They look at him with disdain for what he did and did not do. They use him as an example of someone who almost always said the wrong thing.

As a result, I can't help but feel for the guy. I mean, I would not want generations of absolute strangers knowing about so many of my greatest failures. Yet, since he himself was transparent and real about his life, I am drawn to find out more about Simon Peter (or "Cephas," if you speak Aramaic).

Simon Peter was from the town of Bethsaida, which means "house of the fisherman," where he lived with his wife and family in a decent-sized house on the northern coast of the Sea of Galilee. Living in that region meant he had a strong Galilean accent, the type of accent that told people immediately where he was from—just like you can tell when someone is from Brooklyn or Mississippi. Peter lived in an upper-middle-class community, a mixed neighborhood of Jews and Greeks who worked long hours in the fishing industry. Like most Jewish boys, Peter went to religious school. There, he eventually studied under a teacher known as John the Baptist.

And then Jesus invaded his life. Jesus met Peter and a few of his buddies while they were doing what they always did: fishing. Soon Peter became one of Christ's closest friends. He listened as Jesus gave some remarkable speeches and watched up close and personal as the Lord performed some spectacular miracles. Because of the three years he spent in Christ's physical presence, Peter's life and career as a fisherman were never the same.

The gospel writers have given us plenty of details to piece together a fair assessment of Peter's personality and character—arguably more information than for any other follower of Christ. What these details reveal, however, is much more than a symbol of spiritual failure. In fact, throughout Peter's interactions with Christ and with the early church, we discover a man who seems very familiar to us. Peter could easily be the guy next door or the face we see in the mirror: honest, lively, hard working, genuinely wanting to do the right thing, but clumsy in his attempts. In Peter we see ourselves.

In other words, the more we look at Peter's life, the more we discover a bigger, more amazing picture of just how human and how holy he was. Peter was not a superspiritual Christian who always got it right. Nor was he a brilliant theologian, a religious giant, or a sacrificial saint—just like most of us, no matter how hard we try. Peter's sincere efforts and multiple shortcomings show us the "real" Peter and invite us into a fellowship of equally imperfect believers: sinful but loved, needy but saved, dying but promised life everlasting.

Peter admonishes us to endure our own inconsistencies as we struggle to reflect our consistent Creator. He reminds us that we are part of a community of honest believers who know we are accepted by God and who try to love Him in return but don't always get it right. His life teaches us that God works in and through us—in spite of us—to proclaim the good news of Christ to others: God loves sinners.

Just as we learn about the protagonist of a story through his interactions with other minor characters, we can't help but learn more about the person of Jesus Christ through Peter. Yes, in the weak person of Peter, we get a glimpse of the strength of Jesus. We can know Christ better because we watch in the Scriptures how gracious, firm, and inviting He always was with Peter. We can comprehend His patience because of how patient He was with Peter. And because Peter is the perfect example of imperfection, we can understand more clearly how a Perfect Carpenter from Nazareth can transform a wimpy, wavering soul into a rock.

Like Peter, I want to learn what it means to love Jesus while I walk and smell and hear the world in this crazy earthly body. Just like the fisherman, I want to taste the salt of the sea and be reminded of Christ's great commission to be salt to the earth. I want to find Jesus doing the impossible, even after I argue with Him over how I think it should be done. I want to learn from Peter what it means to be a holy vessel for Christ's purposes, while I also try to be fully responsive and alive as a human being.

Peter might have been more shocked than anyone that he was the one disciple on whom Christ said He would build His church. But when we look at the many sides of Peter's character—good and bad—we recognize him as a leading example of the struggle for faith that every Christian faces, the personal battle each of us confronts daily: Who really is Lord of our lives?

As G. K. Chesterton wrote in his book *Heretics,* Peter was the ideal candidate for building God's church:

> When Christ at a symbolic moment was establishing His great society, He chose for its cornerstone neither the brilliant Paul nor the mystic John, but a shuffler, a snob, a coward—in a word, a man. And upon this rock He has built His Church, and the gates of Hell have not prevailed against it. All the empires and the kingdoms have failed, because of this inherent and continual weakness, that they were founded by strong men and upon strong men. But this one thing, the historic Christian Church, was founded on a weak man, and for that reason it is indestructible. For no chain is stronger than its weakest link.

In the chapters that follow, we'll walk with Peter through many parts of his life, with the hope of seeing him come "alive" on each page. We will follow him chronologically through the Scriptures as he interacts with Jesus, the disciples, and the church, and we'll watch him as he struggles, learns, and grows. Each story will raise several questions as to how Peter can influence our own friendship with Christ and one another. Spend as much time with each question as you like, reflecting privately or exploring corporately the various issues this dynamic biblical character brings to light for us. There's no need to hurry through the questions; sometimes the more we reflect on something, the more we taste its many flavors.

You'll also notice quotations at the beginning and the end of each chapter that provide additional insights about Peter—"bookends" that anchor our discoveries in literary truths. Many of these quotes come directly from children's stories because I believe Peter's life and faith were often childlike in nature and, therefore, full of wisdom. (You might want to read these quotes aloud. Better still, read the stories aloud as a fun supplement to your study of Peter.) Other quotes are from Christian leaders, further exploring the intellectual side of the apostle and helping us make sense of the Christian life.

From each quotation, question, and encounter, we'll see a little more of the complexity of this passionate, imperfect follower of Jesus, and in the process, we'll understand a little more of what it means for us to follow Jesus as well. From Galilean fisherman to enthusiast, denier, missionary, leader, bishop, and, eventually, martyr, Peter took an astonishing journey with Jesus. And we will do well to pay attention.

✍ QUESTION FOR REFLECTION

What is it about Peter that makes you want to study his life and character?

✍ *Indicates further information in Leader's Notes*

ONE

CALLED FOR A CALLING: PETER'S PURPOSE

MARK 1:14-20; LUKE 5:1-11

"Speak your thought, Human Child," said the Lion.

"I was wondering—I mean—could there be some mistake?
Because nobody called me and Scrubb, you know. It was we who
asked to come here. Scrubb said we were to call to—to Somebody—
it was a name I wouldn't know—and perhaps the Somebody
would let us in. And we did and then we found the door open."

"You would not have called to me unless I had been calling to
you," said the Lion.

"Then you are Somebody, Sir?" said Jill.

"I am. And now hear your task."

—C. S. LEWIS, *The Silver Chair*,
The Chronicles of Narnia

It was an exhausting day. For eight hours my mother and I—along with the tour group of thirty senior citizens she was leading—stood on the deck of a ferry that took us through the natural wonders of New Zealand's Milford Sound. In the pouring rain we held on to the deck railing, trying to click cameras at the dozens of waterfalls, seals, and rock formations we passed. This was one of those special tours that whirled you through parts of Australia and New Zealand in record time. Because my mom was the travel escort, I was able to come along for free to see the sights down under and spend some time with her. What I hadn't anticipated, though, was how much energy I would need to keep up with these seniors!

The Milford Sound excursion came after ten days of lectures, museum tours, and guided walks in five different cities and towns. This day—with its gray mountains and rocky waterfalls—was astonishingly beautiful, even if I was drenched and chilled through most of it. When we finally returned to our little motel in Queenstown, I just wanted a hot shower and a bed. I wasn't expecting a lesson about my calling in life.

In between showering and bed, though, I turned on the television. On one of those eight-inch, black-and-white sets, I found only one channel, and its reception looked like a snowstorm had collided with whatever show was airing. I turned up the volume and was amazed to hear Maria in *The Sound of Music*. As I sat on the edge of the bed, all of a sudden— really, it was as if someone had smacked the set—the picture was clearer and brighter than the day I had just spent outside. My eyes opened wide. And for the next few minutes, I marveled as I watched Mother Superior tell a lovesick Maria, "You have to find what you were born for. You have to 'Climb ev'ry mountain, ford ev'ry stream, follow ev'ry rainbow, 'till... you...find...your...dream!'" Then, as if on cue, the set returned to snow at exactly the moment Mother Superior finished her song.

I rubbed my eyes, wondering if I had just seen right. I flipped off the television, got back into bed, and laughed at the bizarre connection I had just experienced. Mountains, streams, and rainbows from the day at Milford Sound flashed through my mind, but Mother Superior's invitation "to find what you were born for" stayed with me the rest of the trip. And it is a question that has lingered with me ever since.

BREAKING GROUND

What effect does the challenge to "find what you were born for" have on you at this time in your life?

GO FISH

It's been ten years since that surprising New Zealand encounter with *The Sound of Music,* and after many discussions and much reflection, I have come to appreciate the Mother's challenge more than ever. She helped me distinguish between being called and having a calling.

I will always remember the first time I "heard" Jesus call me into a relationship with Him. He invited me to come to Him, to bring my burdens to Him as He promised to give me rest. Then He instilled in me the faith to respond—He still does—and I have been fascinated by His presence ever since. In fact, in spite of the things I like to clutter my life with, I believe He continues to call me first and foremost to *Himself*—in prayer, in Bible study, in service, and in relationship with others.

From this place with Jesus comes a specific calling, a purpose, a vocation for which He has uniquely designed me. I have come to believe my own calling is that of an educator, using the tools of teaching and writing in hopes of fulfilling the mission God has imparted to me. Frederick Buechner said, "The place God calls you to is the place where your deep gladness and the world's deep hunger meet." When I operate in this vocation of writing, for instance, I experience a deep gladness that I hope provides some nourishment for the world's deep hunger. Likewise, I believe that in nurturing an intimate connection with our Creator, each child of God discovers his or her unique calling. In Him, we discover what we're born for.

And this is exactly why Peter's life story is so helpful for us. By all external purposes, it seemed Peter's vocation was that of a fisherman. His father was a fisherman, his friends were fishermen, and the typical job for Jew and Greek alike in Bethsaida was that of—you guessed it—fishing. It was the industry that supported the economy of Peter's town, and it afforded him the opportunity to provide for his middle-class family. Fishing was the only work Peter ever knew. But was it what he was born for?

When Jesus came onto the scene, Peter questioned his career options for the first time. The story of Peter's initial interaction with Christ (recorded in Mark 1:14-20 and Luke 5:1-11) provides us with some interesting clues for distinguishing between being called and having a calling. First, Peter had just spent a terrible night at sea. It had been worthless by his standards because his nets were empty—not a good thing for a fisherman. By the time the sun came up, he was probably scratching his head as to how he was going to pay his bills or what he was going to tell his family when he got home.

Then Peter noticed some commotion on shore, and when Jesus called out to him, Peter recognized His voice. It is likely he had heard Jesus preach a few other times before. But what Peter didn't realize was that the Lord was asking him to do something that would prepare him for what lay ahead. Christ suggested he toss out his nets in a different direction, foreshadowing how, instead of fishing the seas, Peter would fish for men's souls. First, though, he had to hear Christ's invitation to come to Him.

I am amazed at how all of history was quite literally affected because of Christ's personal call, or invitation, to Peter and the unique calling on his life that resulted. Peter would go on to climb mountains and ford streams for the sake of the gospel. If Peter had dreams before, well, now they went beyond all he could ever have imagined.

Read the story of Peter's calling in Mark 1:14-20 and Luke 5:1-11.

First Looks

1. What was Peter's initial response when Christ told him to cast his nets one more time?

2. How did Peter respond to Jesus when the nets filled with so many fish? What do Peter's actions and words tell you about his personality and character?

3. Peter and his friends had just brought in the catch of a lifetime, a catch that could catapult their careers. What did they do with it? What does their action say to us?

4. What do you think is the meaning of the verse "Come…and I will make you fishers of men" (Mark 1:17)?

THE ADVENTURE BEGINS

When Maria in *The Sound of Music* discovered what she was born for, it affected many other people as well. The von Trapp children and, of course, the captain himself, were enchanted by her love and commitment; they became a family in the process—and the world gained a classic film.

Peter, too, discovered an entirely new way of life when he first heard the Messiah call his name, and as a result of this call on his life, he entered vocational—or full-time—ministry. His journey would take him in directions he never could have dreamed of: a confidant of the Lord, a leader of God's church, and, finally, a martyr who died a brutal death.

When a person is first called to Jesus, it doesn't necessarily mean that he or she will leave an existing career for full-time ministry. It does mean that every part of his or her life will be affected by a new relationship with Christ, and that, of course, will affect how he or she views career, money, social life, you name it. The gospel penetrates every part of our lives and radically challenges us in the process.

Responding to God's call to follow Him, however, is not always easy, and it is hardly ever what we expect. In our contemporary age many of us fall into the trap of trying to reduce the journey of faith to a simple formula: If we do this spiritual deed, then that "blessing" will happen. If I go to church enough or say this prayer a hundred times, then God will "owe" me, and I will have what I want.

Nothing, of course, could be further from the Person of Truth. If anything, life with the living God is never something we enter on our own terms. It is a mystery where—as Peter discovered—the only predictable element is God's faithfulness. In fact, I find that the older I get, the less I even attempt to understand this adventure I'm on as a Christian. I've all but given up trying to plan my life because when I do, I usually hear—if I'm listening, that is—the Master saying, "No, child, this way."

So instead of keeping control of our lives and careers, we need to hear the One who calls us to Himself and points us in a sometimes new, but always right, direction for His kingdom purposes.

TAKING IT IN

5. Who else—besides Peter—did Jesus call in these two Scripture passages? What does this say about community?

6. Let's look at the definitions of some of the words in the verse "Come, follow me...and I will make you fishers of men" (Mark 1:17). *Come* is a command that suggests a journey. What else could it mean? What do you think of when you hear the word *follow?*

 7. Notice the personal pronoun that Jesus used after the word *follow.* What does that suggest about Jesus and His call? What was He calling Peter to? What *wasn't* He calling him to?

8. Jesus made Peter and his partners a promise in this passage. What was the promise, and which word suggests that it is firm? What did that promise tell the fishermen about their new calling?

9. Next, notice how Christ took responsibility for His disciples' new vocation by saying that *He* would make them fishers of men. How would this take the pressure off them?

CREATIVE WORKS

Ever since that first week when God created the earth, He has shown Himself to be the Maker of beautiful things. God made Peter into a fisher of men, a leader of His people, and a model of a real disciple, that is, someone who was flawed but radically inspired. God never discarded or ignored Peter's unique personality or individuality. If anything, the Almighty used all of Peter's talents and foibles for His purposes, enhancing Peter's strengths and gifts and redeeming his weaknesses to accomplish His plan.

To create is to mold something from nothing. This is God's nature. Since humans are made in His image, we, too, are creative beings called to be cocreators with our Creator. God's intentions are to mold our lives, callings, and artistic efforts for the beauty of the world—just as He did with Peter. I believe He wants each of us to look for ways we can use our creative gifts to honor Him and to better appreciate what it means to be human beings made in God's image, called to Him in intimate fellowship, and gifted with a wonderfully unique calling.

MAKING IT REAL

✒ 10. Christ invited Peter to leave his old way of life and work in order to follow Him. He called Peter to Himself (in relationship), but He also gave him a new calling (or vocation). How does such a personal call speak to you in light of your current lifework or career choices?

11. Peter's response to Christ in Luke 5:11 was immediate and could have been interpreted by some as "irresponsible." What does Peter's passion and his abandon to the person and purposes of Christ teach you?

12. Peter left a familiar lifestyle for one that was completely unknown. Yet following Jesus proved a greater adventure than he could ever have imagined. What adventure is Christ leading you on right now? What is your specific calling?

Ask God to call you to Himself each day, to give you ears to hear His voice and the passion to follow Him wherever He may lead you.

The Greek word for church, *ekklesia*—from *ek* = out, and *kaleo* = call—indicates that as a Christian community we are people who together are called out of familiar places to unknown territories, out of our ordinary and proper places to the places where people hurt and where we can experience with them our common human brokenness and our common need for healing.

—HENRI NOUWEN, DONALD MCNEILL, and DOUGLAS MORRISON,
Compassion: A Reflection on the Christian Life

RAW PASSION:
WALKING TO JESUS

MATTHEW 14:22-33; 16:13-23

*"But, I don't understand," said Dorothy in bewilderment. "How
was it that you appeared to me as a great Head?"*

*"That was one of my tricks," answered Oz. "Step this way,
please, and I will tell you all about it."*

—FRANK BAUM, *The Wonderful World of Oz*

Life is seldom what it seems. When I was growing up, for instance, I
dreamed of being an Olympic athlete. When I graduated from college, I
expected to be a high-school English teacher for the rest of my days on
earth. And when I settled into a downtown neighborhood, I was certain
I would live there forever.

Now, several bruises, "careers," and apartments later, I am convinced
that within the adventure we call "living," the only certainty we can trust
is God's faithful presence to accompany us on the journey. Our dreams
change, new relationships arise, and opportunities come and go. What we
once seemed confident about or familiar with often took a twist in the road
we never saw coming and we were left groping for a Hand to guide us.

Obviously, we humans are creatures of comfort, and so these changes in our lives can feel like dark storms to endure rather than opportunities to grow. And if you are like me, you know that when such windy circumstances blow our way, they bring out both the best and the worst in us. Our excitement about a new job, a new friendship, or a new city, quickly deteriorates into fear or anxiety as reality hits: How'd we get into this in the first place? What *were* we thinking?

BREAKING GROUND

What twists or turns has your life adventure taken lately?

WAVES OF FEAR

If ever there was a man who rode the waves of his emotions from one extreme to another, whose life of comfort and familiarity was regularly disrupted, it was Peter. Here was a follower of Christ whose passion for living flipped between sheer enthusiasm and absolute terror—often within seconds! It wasn't that Peter was unfamiliar with the challenge of change or the precarious storms of life; in fact, they dictated his life as a fisherman. But in what is probably his second greatest claim to fame—his walk on the water found in Matthew 14:29-30—Peter provides us with a perfect picture of human inconsistency in the light of our Lord's constancy.

Imagine the scene: Peter and the other disciples had just watched (from inches away, no doubt) Jesus heal dozens of sick people and feed a crowd of over five thousand with only five loaves of bread and two fish. His miraculous provision was so generous that the disciples picked up twelve basketfuls of leftovers. Understandably, Jesus wanted to rest a bit, so He sent His disciples on ahead of Him while He dismissed the crowd and then spent some time alone praying on a mountainside.

Who knows what Peter and his pals must have been feeling in the boat that night after seeing with their own eyes Christ's astonishingly supernatural deeds. Were they energized from the day's amazing events? Were they exuberant about the marvelous acts they had witnessed? They might have been, but according to the gospel account, it seems that they didn't have much time to revel in their emotions. They soon found themselves in the middle of the lake with a terrible wind blowing around them. It was so terrible, in fact, that these experienced fishermen had to focus all their attention on keeping the boat on course. Water flew across the deck, tossing the small motorless fishing boat around like a ball. The sky darkened, and even though the veteran fishermen had likely endured this type of weather before, they struggled to battle the forces of nature. They held on. And they waited.

At around three in the morning, they saw something moving across the water, and they could hardly believe their eyes. Terror set in. Was it a ghost? Certainly, the possibility of a ghost was more frightening to them than the storm, because at least they had seen stormy weather before. They had endured crashing waves and terrific winds. But a phantom walking on water? That was the last thing they expected, and the very prospect was horrifying.

Read Matthew 14:22-33.

FIRST LOOKS

1. Why was Jesus walking across the lake?

2. What do you think motivated Peter's bold request to Jesus? Why do you think Jesus invited him to come out on the water?

3. How was Peter able to walk on the water? What do his actions say about his personality?

4. What did the disciples conclude after Jesus and Peter got into the boat? What did that mean for them?

RISKY WATERS

When Jesus walked out to that boat, He was already familiar with the terrors of storms—both the natural kind and the human kind. Participating in the sovereign fellowship with His Father and the Holy Spirit, Jesus had long ago experienced a flood that engulfed the entire planet; He had endured the plagues and earthquakes and storms that destroyed entire nations. And He had witnessed people destroying one another in battle after battle. When He entered the earth as a babe, the King of glory was familiar with violence, intimate with suffering, and painfully aware of storms of all kinds. They did not surprise Him, nor did they intimidate Him.

But what was just an evening stroll for Jesus was a horror film for His disciples. That is, until Peter responded in typical fashion: He recognized who the "ghost" was and actually climbed overboard, boat rocking, waves crashing! Passion overcame all logic and, as usual, the experienced fisherman followed his heart, not his head. In fact, he intuitively responded in the midst of the disaster and ignored all the laws of nature—until, of course, he was out of the boat. That's when his head took over.

Wait a minute, he must have thought in a panic, as he *stood* there on the water. *This defies nature. People don't walk on water. In fact, this is dangerous. I could drown out here. What* was *I thinking?* Obviously, Peter was *not* thinking when he first walked toward Jesus. Not that using his mind was not important. But the minute he let conventional wisdom rather than a heart full of desire dictate his steps toward Jesus, doubt entered the picture and he began to think—quite dramatically—that he was sinking. It is the classic example of how we can look at our circumstances and be overwhelmed instead of fixing our eyes on the One who controls them.

How quickly this fisherman called to Jesus from the boat. How quickly he then climbed overboard to pursue Him—in a storm, no less. And how quickly he was overcome by doubt, his face wet from the waves that now blocked his vision of the One he was going after in the first place.

There he was, in the middle of a windy lake in the middle of the night, *standing* on top of the water. He started to shake in fear at exactly the same time he *realized* he was in the middle of a windy lake in the middle of the night, *standing* on top of the water. What happened next is a beautiful example of Christ's character and His mission. As verse 31 says, "Immediately Jesus reached out his hand and caught him." Grace, salvation, and compassion personified in one extended hand.

In other words, Christ was not—and is not—in the habit of calling His friends into seemingly impossible situations only to let them drown. I love how this simple exchange not only shows us Peter's passionate desire to live fully with Jesus but reveals Christ's longing for us to do so as well. Here's what I mean: When Peter said, "Lord, if it's you...tell me to come to you on the water" (verse 28), Jesus could have said, "Ah, well, Peter, it's dangerous out here. You had better stay put where it's nice and safe and predictable." Instead, the Lord invited His well-meaning disciple to "Come," that is, to step out of his perceived place of comfort and safety into a potentially frightening, out-of-the-ordinary experience where any-thing—literally—was possible. His invitation to risk and take a step toward adventure was anchored in the promise of His presence.

And that was good news for Peter—as it is for those of us who want to live abundantly, take risks, and experience the goodness of God, all in the same breath! Because Peter's initial faith was active and daring rather than passive and safe, Jesus rewarded him with the ride of his life. But what is perhaps more exciting still is the fact that even after Peter stepped out into the unknown and started to waver, Christ offered His hand. He saved Peter. Christ pulled him out of the danger of his doubts and into the protection of His faithfulness. And He does it time and time again for His children.

Anyone who encounters the person of Jesus Christ is in a position to watch his or her life be turned upside down and his or her priorities re-defined—as Peter did. The Prince of Peace has a way of uprooting our self-made values and belief systems and leading us down a completely new road that is always better than the old ways and is certainly healthier for us. I can't pretend that the process of such a conversion means smooth sailing, but eventually we come to experience the Almighty's calming our personal storms, healing our wounds, and restoring our dignity—each act a miracle that draws us closer to Him.

The storm that night was never, well, a storm for Jesus. The storms of life still aren't. Though He of course grieves over every storm in our lives, He never moves away from us in the midst of them. In the same way He walked toward His disciples as the waves crashed against their boat, knowing their fears and even calling one brave soul to step out of the boat into a seemingly impossible event, He walks toward us, revealing His character of compassion and His constant commitment to relationship with us.

TAKING IT IN

5. What happened to the wind when Jesus and Peter got into the boat together? What do you think this could mean?

6. How do you think Peter's perception of Jesus was affected by this remarkable experience?

7. How does this true adventure story expand your definition of the word *faith?*

Read Matthew 16:13-23.

STILL STORMS

In the middle of the lake that night—before he began to doubt, that is—Peter must have had a sense of just who he was walking toward. He must have known in his bones—if only for a moment—that God Himself was standing on the water, inviting Peter to join Him. And so, a few adventures after their lake-walk, when Jesus asked Peter, "Who do you say I am?" (verse 15), Peter's memory was fresh and his faith full. He had also just witnessed another miraculous feeding of the multitudes and several more miraculous healings. Zealous to please his leader, Simon Peter answered, "You are the Christ, the Son of the living God" (verse 16). And for once he got it right.

His confession, however, did not come—as we might expect—because of his own religious knowledge or experience with Jesus. Neither did he "get it" because the other disciples convinced him. Instead, Peter understood just who Jesus was because "this was not revealed to you by man, but by my Father in heaven" (verse 17). Though Peter was pushy, impulsive, and often precocious, God was delighted to reveal His truth to the brash fisherman. Nothing pleases the Father more than when His children—and Peter was certainly a big child—are willing to receive, when they have ears to hear and eyes to see His gifts.

Then, in another remarkable change of direction, Jesus gave Simon Peter a new identity, a new name, a new purpose. And as He did, He empowered him for this role: "I tell you that you are Peter, and on this rock I will build my church, and the gates of Hades will not overcome it" (verse 18). Peter, a *rock?* The guy who almost drowned getting out of a boat in the middle of a lake? Build the church on *him?* Just because he gave the right answer?

Absolutely. For it was Peter's sincerity of heart that Christ loved, not his ability to get it right. It was Peter's passionate spirit Christ enjoyed, not his expertise as a fisherman. This exchange reveals to us Christ's intentions to build His church, fulfill His purposes, and reach the world through fickle humans to whom God reveals Himself. And that gives me, as an equally fickle human, great encouragement. We have only to step toward Jesus, acknowledge who He is, and expect the unexpected!

MAKING IT REAL

8. A person's identity and purpose undergo a transformation when he or she comes to recognize who Christ is. Reflect for a moment on how professing faith in Jesus can change someone. Has it changed you? In what ways?

9. How does Christ's new purpose for Peter encourage you in your purpose?

10. What risks could you take to step closer to Jesus? What might be keeping you "in the boat"?

11. When have you seen Jesus "walking on the water" to get to you in the midst of a storm in your life?

✂ 12. Peter's passion played a crucial role in his miraculous adventure. What are you passionate about?

Ask God to make you more aware of His presence as you pursue your passions.

> Out in front of us is the drama of men and of nations, seething, struggling, laboring, dying. Upon this tragic drama in these days our eyes are all set in anxious watchfulness and in prayer. But within the silences of the souls of men an eternal drama is ever being enacted, in these days as well as in others. And on the outcome of this inner drama rests, ultimately, the outer pageant of history.
>
> —THOMAS R. KELLY, *The Shepherd in Search of Lost Obedience*

PRECOCIOUS INNOCENCE: THE MOUNT OF TRANSFIGURATION

MATTHEW 17:1-13; MARK 9:2-10; LUKE 9:28-36

After one glance at the Lion's feet he slipped out of the saddle and fell at its feet. He couldn't say anything but then he didn't want to say anything, and he knew he needn't say anything. The High King above all kings stooped toward him. Its mane, and some strange and solemn perfume that hung about the mane, was all round him. It touched his forehead with its tongue. He lifted his face and their eyes met. Then instantly the pale brightness of the mist and the fiery brightness of the Lion rolled themselves together into a swirling glory and gathered themselves up and disappeared.

—C. S. LEWIS, *The Horse and His Boy,*
The Chronicles of Narnia

About a year ago I was working as a writer for an Ivy League university. I enjoyed the variety of stories I was able to write for the faculty newspaper about scholars barely thirty years old, excelling in their fields; journalism professors writing plays instead of articles; students running a radio station so they could interview artists and filmmakers. There was no shortage of interesting people, events, and ideas for me to cover.

There was also no shortage of ego for a few of the administrators, professors, and students there. This was, after all, a world-class institution that prided itself on groundbreaking research, expert analyses, and cutting-edge technology, a place that poured thousands of dollars into promoting its own reputation while improving its existing programs. Who could argue that it did indeed provide a remarkable educational opportunity for students and scholars alike?

With such intellectual aptitude and academic excellence, you would think that few people working at this university would have reason to feel insignificant, afraid, or insecure. But when news of a new president spread, many of my colleagues ran for cover. What would they have to do to keep their jobs in this new regime? And many wondered if they would have to prove themselves all over again, in spite of their impeccable contributions to the university community, when the new president actually arrived on campus with his own team of administrators. Would they survive the inevitable crises that come with leadership changes, or would they have to compromise their integrity in order to stay?

Breaking Ground

Describe a time in your life when you witnessed a struggle (or conflict) for personal or professional power.

WHO'S THE *REAL* BOSS?

The questions—and the fears—around the water cooler, I have to confess, astounded me. I was amazed to see usually confident individuals genuinely worried about their jobs, second-guessing themselves even though they had stellar track records. Some put their résumés together "just in case," they told me; others turned in their resignation letters because they didn't want to risk getting fired, though they'd done nothing wrong. Maybe I was missing something, but I just couldn't figure out what all the frenzy was about.

The apostle Peter—as usual—helped me "get it." One morning as I read about his encounter with Christ, Moses, and Elijah on the Mount of Transfiguration (see Matthew 17:1-13; Mark 9:2-10; and Luke 9:28-36), I began to understand what was happening around me: Because people perceived this "world-class institution" as the ultimate authority in their lives and their primary source of provision and opportunity, they weren't sure what to do when it started to change. As this familiar foundation appeared to crumble, setting in place its own "transfiguration," they got anxious. Simply put, they felt there was no bigger authority to trust. That in turn triggered a classic survival instinct, one that tempted even the most capable people to take matters into their own hands as they tried to gain some sense of control.

At first glance, Peter's experience on the Mount of Transfiguration might not seem to correlate specifically with this Ivy League scenario or with similar situations we might face. But let's look at the story. The gospel writers first show us Jesus reminding His disciples—again—that, "The Son of Man must suffer many things and be rejected by the elders, chief priests and teachers of the law, and he must be killed and on the third day be raised to life" (Luke 9:22). Obviously, Christ was preparing His followers for the stark reality that their leadership was about to go through some monumental changes, and it wasn't going to be easy for anyone involved.

A little over a week after He warned the disciples of His horrendous destiny—and after they had witnessed several additional miracles of healing and provision—Christ grabbed three close friends—Peter, John, and James—and hiked up a mountain to pray. As Jesus began praying, "the appearance of his face changed, and his clothes became as bright as a flash of lightning" (Luke 9:29), and the book of Mark describes His clothes as "dazzling white, whiter than anyone in the world could bleach them" (9:3). The detail isn't there, but I think it's safe to assume Peter and his pals were not looking at the trees or the wildflowers at this point; their Leader was once again doing something altogether new and unfamiliar to them. He was shining. Glowing. He was radiant as "a flash of lightning," and I suspect they could not take their eyes off Him.

As if that weren't enough to keep their attention, suddenly a team of Jesus' personal "administrators"—Moses and Elijah, who were also shining in "glorious splendor" (Luke 9:31)—appeared on the scene to visit the Lord. In fact, they had a good discussion about His ensuing departure or exodus (a term Moses was quite familiar with), and this, too, was an uncommonly bright moment.

As an educated Jewish boy, Peter was certainly aware of the stories of Moses and Elijah. He knew of their intimate walks with God, their bold leadership qualities, and how both had pointed their people to the coming Messiah. Peter knew that glory on mountaintops was to Moses and Elijah a familiar experience, only this time others were allowed to watch.

Then Peter, with his usual impulsiveness, and with what I'm sure was the utmost innocence, told Jesus—he did not ask—that it was a really good thing he and the other two disciples had come along. Why? Because now he could use his knowledge and skills to build each of the three biblical leaders a permanent shelter by which to remember them. He could impress them. And that might be a good thing for Peter since he wasn't sure just how—or if—this new leadership structure might define itself now that Moses and Elijah were here. He certainly wasn't going to run the risk of getting edged out of his place as one of Christ's confidants. He did not want to lose his significance, nor did he want to get reassigned.

So Peter resorted to an old defense mechanism he used whenever he felt a bit insecure: He put the focus back on himself. He tried to regain a sense of control. Instead of eavesdropping on what was likely one of the most fascinating conversations in all of history, Peter began to squirm. Instead of quietly observing this miraculous gathering of God's prophets, he got a little uncomfortable and decided to take things into his own hands. Peter then told Jesus what he could do for Him.

Read the three accounts of the Mount of Transfiguration in Matthew 17:1-13, Mark 9:2-10, and Luke 9:28-36.

FIRST LOOKS

1. What specific details from each account give you a clear picture of the event?

2. What classic symbols from the Old Testament do you see in this story? How do they help link the Hebrew Scriptures to Christ?

3. What do you suppose was the purpose of the Transfiguration? For whose benefit was it?

4. Why do you think Jesus appeared in dazzling white?

The Ultimate Mountaintop

During this mountaintop experience, Peter forgot one thing: He did not ultimately control his personal circumstances. No matter how much ability he had, how many degrees he earned, or how many rabbis (or college presidents) he knew, Peter—like all of us—was not the captain of his own ship. There was—and is—an Authority that reigned above any human plans Peter might make, a Sovereignty that ruled all earthly situations he found himself in, and a Power that transcended even world-class earthly endeavors. God Almighty, the Creator of the universe, was—and is—in charge.

In His grace, God did not zap His well-meaning disciple out of existence for wrongly believing the three men before him were equals. Peter did not get fired, nor did he get relegated to another department. Instead, the brilliant and impenetrable presence of God appeared in a cloud—as it had with Moses hundreds of years before—to set the record straight. And from the cloud came a Voice. *The* Voice. The Ultimate Authority demand-ing that the now-terrified Peter understand just *who* it was he had been following. Christ was not merely another religious leader, nor was He only a spiritual orator or righteous prophet. No, this was "my Son, whom I have chosen; listen to him" (Luke 9:35).

And Peter—puny, humbled, knees shaking—fell on his face in proper fear of the One who keeps the earth spinning, the One who actually gov-erns human life. He could not help but listen. In the process, Peter moved a little closer to understanding the Power that is beyond all powers. His name is Jesus.

Matthew's description of what happened next on the mountain is another beautiful reminder of Christ's paradoxical nature: He is both ten-der and sovereign, Servant and Ruler, Lamb and Lion. For as Peter and his friends lay quivering in terror at the Voice they'd just heard loud and clear, "Jesus came and touched them" (Matthew 17:7). Certainly, He did not have to do this. He could have simply ordered His followers to get it together and act like adults. I mean really, three grown men—His top leaders no less—sniffling and shivering face down in the dirt could have been an embarrassment for Jesus. In front of Elijah and Moses at that.

But Jesus calmed their very human fear with His God-in-the-flesh presence. He touched them. He spoke to the insecurity that had paralyzed them by telling them to take action, to "get up." And He encouraged their souls with a gentle command, "Don't be afraid."

By now, Peter's head must have been swirling. As we read in chapter 2, shortly before their mountaintop encounter, Peter had rightly recognized Jesus as the Christ, the Messiah who would save His people from their sins (see Matthew 16:16). It had been revealed to him then by the same Voice he now heard on the mountain. But just as quickly as Peter got it right, he turned around and—with the best of intentions, I'm sure—got it really wrong.

Taking It In

5. Jesus had a discussion on the mountain with Moses and Elijah. What was significant about these two Old Testament prophets?

6. What does Christ's response to the disciples on the mountain reveal to you about their relationship?

7. Jesus gave His disciples orders not to tell anyone what they had seen until after He had risen from the dead. Why do you think He did this? What did such a statement about His destiny communicate to them?

8. Look at Mark 8:31–9:1, the passage just before the account of the Transfiguration. Why do you suppose Jesus talked about

taking up His cross before He went to the mountain to pray? Why do you suppose Peter "rebuked" Jesus (8:32)? How do you think Peter felt when Christ in turn rebuked him? Can you relate to Peter's actions? Explain.

MOVING UP

A chapter earlier in Mark, we read that when Jesus revealed to His followers how He was to die, Peter's impulsive, comfort-loving self challenged his Lord's authority, "took him aside and began to rebuke him" (Mark 8:32). Amazing! How quickly the fisherman forgot just whom he was with!

Jesus—smelling a bad egg—in turn rebuked Peter: "Get behind me, Satan!... You do not have in mind the things of God, but the things of men" (Mark 8:33). Thankfully, Christ knew that His enemy was not Peter, but Satan, that the cross He spoke of was both His mission to bring salvation and His message to His followers about how to live (see Mark 8:34). For Peter, however—as for most of us—that reality would take awhile to sink in.

So when Peter heard a Voice on the mountain rebuking him again, when he knew he had blown it again, he naturally was afraid. Human nature expects the worst in times like this, not a calming touch of forgiveness or a word of hope that says, "Get up. Don't be afraid." Such personal attention was a pattern Peter was getting used to.

Once Peter and the others were confident enough to lift their heads from the ground, they saw no one but Jesus. The other figures—Moses and Elijah—did not remain with the disciples, because they were not able to make the promise Jesus went on to make after He suffered: "Surely I am with you always" (Matthew 28:20). No historic icon, no contemporary hero, no human being, regardless of how important he or she is to us, can make such a promise. Only the Son of God can—and did.

The promise of Jesus' presence, then, ought to develop in us a deep trust in His provision and care. For if Jesus Christ is who He said He is, we have no reason to worry about how we might pay the rent or whether new leadership at work will threaten our jobs. Throughout the Old and New Testaments, we see time and again our Lord's commitment to caring for His children in ways they could never have imagined, and as the writer of Hebrews reminds us, "Jesus Christ is the same yesterday and today and forever" (13:8). What a marvel for sinners like us that He can and does provide for us exactly what we need when we need it.

Peter's interaction with Jesus both before and after their mountaintop experience reinforces how little we have to say about how and when God acts, only that He will. When Christ came down the mountain, for example, He told Peter, John, and James not to talk about what they had seen until "the Son of Man had risen from the dead" (Mark 9:9). Christ's authority on the matter was clear, and so was His sense of timing. He knew certain events had to happen so the Scriptures might be fulfilled, and waiting through them was an essential part of God's plan.

So it is with us. We do not need to argue with God over what He should do in the future (like Peter did), nor do we need to ramble on and on in our insecurities about what we could do for Him (like Peter did). He invites us instead simply to rest in who He is, to trust in the reality that He reigns over all the earth and that He does so with our best interests in mind.

Even when we—like Peter—get it wrong.

MAKING IT REAL

9. In what ways has God's presence comforted you in anxious times?

10. How has God's provision of grace surprised you lately? Has He "tapped" your shoulder in times when you were afraid or weren't listening to Him? How did you respond?

Reflect for a few moments on the Power above all powers, the Lord above all lords. Thank Him for who He is and ask Him to continue forming in you a deep trust in His authority.

The care of the disciples was care for the day, not for the morrow; the word morrow must stand for any and every point of the future. The next hour, the next moment, is as much beyond our grasp and as much in God's care as that a hundred years away. Care for the next minute is just as foolish as care for the morrow, or for a day in the next thousand years—in neither can we do anything, in both God is doing everything.

—GEORGE MacDONALD, "The Cause of Spiritual Stupidity,"
Unspoken Sermons

FOUR

Rock Bottom: The Last Supper and Peter's Denial

JOHN 12:1-7; 13:1-17; 18:1-11,15-27

A tear, a real tear, trickled down his little shabby velvet nose and fell to the ground.

—MARGERY WILLIAMS, *The Velveteen Rabbit*

You wouldn't recognize his name. But for twenty years a particular author in New York City wrote dozens of books on dozens of subjects. For hundreds of pages, he explored obscure topics such as the various designs of light fixtures, the challenges of winter gardening, and the historic travels of equally obscure people. Each book he was able to sell to a publisher, and each one had, as they say in the publishing industry, a sad and short shelf life. In other words, few people ever bought his books, and fewer still followed his work.

I learned of the author only when I read a newspaper column about him a few months ago. The columnist's kid sister had married the author, and so, year after year he listened to his unpopular brother-in-law explain with great fervor his latest literary endeavor. Every subject fascinated the author; every book project was an adventure in wonder. And now, as the unknown author succumbed to cancer, he was perhaps the most unsuccessful writer of books any columnist could have known. Here was a writer who never became famous for his work, whose books never came close to a spot on the bestseller list. In short, he had failed in his efforts to meet industry standards.

Still, the columnist marveled at the fact that his brother-in-law was also the most passionate human being he'd ever known. He loved writing. And though he expressed disappointment each time one of his books failed, the author never gave up on his vocation. He was content in what he did. Some editors might have labeled this author a failure, but the columnist clearly thought otherwise.

BREAKING GROUND

What do success and failure look like to you?

STATUS SYMBOLS

In a success-driven culture such as ours, failure is the one aspect of life we are instructed to avoid at all costs. Unlike the unknown author, most of us don't yet understand the secret to being content in the midst of perceived failure. We are not satisfied with mediocrity. We want it all. We do not want failure. We do not like to make mistakes. And we certainly never,

ever want to fall to the bottom of whatever career ladder we're trying to climb. No, give us recognition, affirmation, and, of course, success; these are what humans crave.

In the midst of our pursuits, however, it is easy to forget that failure is often our greatest teacher. And Peter's legendary failures offer us some of the most powerful lessons we could ever learn on the subject.

The first lesson is found at the Last Supper. Jesus had gathered His followers in an upper room of a home in Jerusalem to prepare them for what looked like a pretty bleak ending for their King. Talk about a success story gone awry! Certainly, no one who knew better would have expected the majestic Messiah to be defeated on a cross. Nonetheless, Christ's un-imaginable destiny was imminent, and He spent His last night preparing the disciples for what was to come.

What Jesus did, however, once again confounded His friends. Accord-ing to John 13:1-17, He left His place at the head of the table—aware of the shame and agony that awaited Him—wrapped a slave's towel around His waist, and began one of the most menial tasks of the culture at that time: washing the dirty feet of His friends. It was the humiliating work of a servant, not the dignified work of a Master.

Just as Peter had objected to Christ's prediction of His death, he reacted with horror at what his Lord was about to do to his feet. Why? Because Peter was well aware that slaves served their masters, not the other way around. For Jesus to suddenly take on such a disgraceful role turned Peter's thinking upside down—again. Wasn't this a total subversion of authority? Didn't people on the top fight to retain their status in the hier-archy of power and keep those beneath them at bay? If Jesus—the Man Peter left everything to follow—suddenly stooped to foot washing, well, Peter's entire understanding of power—and of the Lord of lords—was threatened.

Naturally, Peter argued with Jesus about what He was about to do. And naturally, Jesus told Peter he didn't yet understand what was about to happen. "But later you will understand" (verse 7), Christ said to His passionate follower. This wasn't quite good enough for the impulsive apostle—delayed gratification is always difficult—and so he bluntly refused the Lord's offer: "No...you shall never wash my feet" (verse 8).

The Lord's gesture, though, was more than an opportunity for Peter to get his feet clean. It was a call to conversion, to accept this upside-down kingdom where the Master voluntarily fell to the bottom of the ladder. It was an invitation to participate in a radical new order in which Jesus—the Ultimate Servant—was the head over all. It also blurred the lines between failure and success for Peter. Unfortunately, he still didn't get it and, in typical form, went to the other extreme.

"Then Lord,...not just my feet but my hands and my head as well," he demanded (verse 9). At this point, I can just imagine the Lord chuckling, sighing, and then taking a long pause as He stood before His obstreperous disciple. Perhaps He gazed long and hard at the guy from Galilee, broke into a delighted smile, and simply went about the business of washing Peter's feet anyway, of "baptizing" His follower with a basin of water, of cleansing the sinful soul of this well-meaning disciple. Thankfully, Peter let Him this time, and, unbeknownst to him, the very act prepared Peter for what would surely be his most despairing encounter with failure—ever.

Yes, if Peter would be associated with his Lord, he must let Him do what He wished. Jesus knew that Peter, His rock, was about to lose his footing, that his faith was about to weaken and lead him into the darkest chaos he would ever know. Yet, even knowing full well that Peter was about to deny Him, Jesus—in a most incredible gesture of love—washed his feet, if for nothing else than to show Peter that no matter how dirty he would get, Jesus would cleanse him. Jesus forgave him.

Read John 12:1-7 and then John 13:1-17.

First Looks

1. What parallels do you see between the two foot-washing stories?

2. What else do you learn about Peter's personality from his interaction with Christ here?

3. Christ knew that Peter was going to deny Him, yet He washed his feet anyway. What does this reveal about the character and love of Jesus?

4. What command did Jesus give the disciples when He had finished washing their feet?

Read John 18:1-11.

THE END'S BEGINNING

After their last supper together had came to a close and Christ had given them the powerful symbols of His body and blood, He looked at His followers and sadly said, "You will all fall away" (Mark 14:27). No matter how much He wanted the contrary, Jesus knew that the coming days would be difficult, despairing, and chaotic for His followers. Their loyalty and faith would be tested in ways they could never have expected.

Peter, of course, was convinced that Jesus was wrong—again. He was as passionate in resisting Christ's prediction as he had been about arguing over whether the Lord would wash his feet. Consider Peter's absolute determination when he first boasted to Jesus, "Even if all fall away on account of you, I never will," (Matthew 26:33), and then, "Even if I have to die with you, I will never disown you" (verse 35). And he wasn't alone in his resolve. Matthew recorded that "all the other disciples said the same" (verse 35).

Luke wrote of Christ's exchange with Peter this way: "'Simon, Simon, Satan has asked to sift you as wheat. But I have prayed for you, Simon, that your faith may not fail. And when you have turned back, strengthen your brothers.' But he replied, 'Lord, I am ready to go with you to prison and to death'" (Luke 22:31-33). And John 13:37-38 says that when Peter asked Jesus, "Lord, why can't I follow you now? I will lay down my life for you," Jesus replied with the echoing words that all of history recalls: "Will you really lay down your life for me? I tell you the truth, before the rooster crows, you will disown me three times!"

The signs were obvious. Yet Peter, though resolute in his devotion to Jesus, had no idea what really was about to happen. He would not believe that Christ's arrest and subsequent murder would come so quickly after their last supper together, and so the ensuing events swirled around him like a storm. He was caught off guard.

Still, Peter was a fighter. When he followed the Lord into the trap

Judas had set, Peter could not control himself. If he had anything to say about it, he would not let the Pharisees arrest his Lord. He would prove his devotion to Jesus, no matter what. He would not fail his Lord. And he would muster all the courage he could to help his Lord succeed.

As Christ's captors invaded the garden, Peter drew his sword and sliced off the right ear of the high priest's servant. Immediately, though, Jesus rendered His final rebuke to His impulsive follower: "Put your sword away! Shall I not drink the cup the Father has given me?" (John 18:10-11). His words marked the turning point for Peter. For as he heard his Lord speak, Peter's own descent began. Down he went into the darkest failure he would ever experience.

Taking It In

5. When Peter and the disciples accompanied Jesus to the garden, He admonished them to pray "so that you will not fall into temptation" (Luke 22:46). Then Christ Himself knelt and prayed. What happened to Him? How did the disciples respond?

6. Peter was sincerely determined to follow Jesus, no matter what. But we know that no matter how hard he tried, he could not do what he said he would. In fact, he failed. What does that suggest about the futility of human effort and our need for God's grace?

7. When Christ was about to be arrested, we saw two kinds of anger expressed. What was the difference between Peter's anger and Christ's?

8. Read Luke 22:47-51. What did Jesus demonstrate by healing the high priest's servant?

Read John 18:15-27.

NIGHTMARE

His head must have been spinning. For three years Peter had given up everything to follow this Man from Nazareth named Jesus. He had listened to His stories and sermons and watched Him feed thousands of people and heal countless diseases; he even experienced the power of the Almighty in ways that defied the laws of nature. Jesus was different from anyone Peter knew. Jesus had loved him. Jesus had offered him hope.

But now that his Lord had been arrested, Peter must have questioned everything he'd experienced. Had he wasted the last three years of his life? Had he been manipulated into believing something that might not be true after all? Had he been a complete fool for trusting the Man who claimed He was the Messiah? It was all so confusing now. His friends had run off when Jesus was arrested, and now Peter was alone. Distraught. Desperate. Doomed to fail.

Aimlessly, Peter wandered around the courtyard, hoping for a last glimpse of Jesus, if only to convince himself that maybe he hadn't been a fool. The night was cold, and he walked toward a fire to warm himself. Emotions ran through his soul. Thoughts jumped in and out of his head. There beside the flames, someone recognized him as a follower of Christ.

He denied it.

Peter stared into the fire. Someone else said, "You are not one of his disciples, are you?" (verse 25). Again, he said no. But when a relative of the man Peter had attacked with his sword saw his face in the light of the blaze, he challenged him, "Didn't I see you with him in the olive grove?" (verse 26).

But Peter still could not speak the truth. He had not lost his courage; he had lost his purpose for living. And when he heard a rooster begin to crow, he remembered the words of his Lord, went outside, and sobbed and sobbed until no tears were left in his emotional, impulsive, well-meaning soul.

At last, Peter came to the truth that he was, in fact, a failure. And that realization would make all the difference.

MAKING IT REAL

9. Why do you think Peter denied knowing Christ? In what ways do modern Christians deny knowing Him?

10. Has there been a time in your life when—like Peter—you felt you had lost your purpose for living, that Christ's call on your life was not very clear? How did you respond?

11. What does the fact that Peter wept bitterly and publicly—outside the courtyard—suggest about his attitude toward his sin?

Spend some moments in confession, acknowledging your sin before God and reflecting on His cleansing grace through Christ's death on the cross.

Is a tired and disillusioned heart any closer to You than a young and happy one? Where can we ever hope to find You, if neither our simple joys nor ordinary sorrows succeed in revealing You to us? Indeed our day-to-day pleasures seem somehow especially designed to make us forget about You, and with our daily disappointments it's no better: they make our hearts so sick and bitter that we seem to lose any talent we ever had for discovering You. O God, it seems we can lose sight of You in anything we do.

—KARL RAHNER, "God of My Daily Routine,"
Encounters with Silence

FIVE

BROKEN FOR GOOD: PETER'S RECOMMISSIONING

JOHN 20:1-9; 21:1-23

Yes, yes, it's really me! And you've already forgiven me, haven't you? Oh dear Father how good you are! And to think that instead I…oh!

—CARLO COLLODI, *Pinocchio*

Icicles hung off the edge of the roof of the chalet. A fresh fall of snow lay beneath them, surrounding the small Swiss home and glistening in the morning sun. I opened the door and stepped into the chill of the mountain air. Mine were the first steps to intrude on the cold white ground this morning as I made my way up the hill to the village.

I was barely twenty years old, disillusioned with both my past and my future and so I had traveled halfway around the world in search of…something. I wasn't sure what. Friends had wanted to backpack in Europe, and I was only too quick to oblige. They mentioned something about a small community in the Swiss Alps run by a Christian thinker I'd never heard of named Francis Schaeffer. But I didn't really care where we went or who was there. I only wanted to leave my college studies—and my life back home.

The memory of this particular snowy morning has lingered with me now for almost twenty years. It's what I consider my first "crisis of faith," that is, a time when questions were more earnest than answers in my head, when chaos was more real than peace in my heart. I had learned of Jesus through a high-school youth organization, announced my faith in Him, and then proceeded to try to "live like a Christian." Now five years later I wasn't sure what that meant, if it meant anything at all. I was full of doubt, not faith.

While others at L'Abri—Schaeffer's Christian community—were reading his books or engaging in intellectual discussions with him, I was studying the Scriptures for the first time. The Prophets and Psalms of the Old Testament, the Gospels and Epistles of the New. Strange words, stranger stories. How did they relate to me? Nothing was breaking through the clouds in my head, so I got up early one morning, put on my coat, and walked through the snow. I wasn't sure where I'd end up because I wasn't sure about anything. I just wanted to go.

I walked through one mountain village and into the next. I wandered into shops, watched skiers, and finally ducked into a café that looked down into the valley. There I sipped coffee and stared out the window, looking at nothing, looking at everything. The decision before me felt heavy: Would I follow Jesus or wouldn't I? Would I live a "Christian life" or wouldn't I? I knew this "Christianity stuff" wasn't a game to play or a mask to wear. I knew I needed to make either an honest attempt or abandon it entirely.

I was writing some of this in a letter to a friend when suddenly words landed gently in my ears: "I have come that [you] may have life, and have it to the full." Jesus' proclamation in John 10:10 surfaced from somewhere in the midst of my confusion, and I was pierced. I knew at that point that

I wanted to live—passionately, fully, abundantly—and if Jesus was the way to abundant life, He was the way I wanted to go.

I left L'Abri a few weeks later with no profound intellectual insights or theological arguments except this: "Jesus loves me. This I know, for the Bible tells me so." And many times since, I have clung to that truth as it became my anchor and once again restored my purpose. It is the truth I returned to as I encountered other "crises of faith" or "breaking years"— those times when I wasn't always certain who or what I believed.

If you have been on the Christian journey, you have probably experienced these moments as well: Stripped of self-righteousness, you see the grip on the idols in your life being pried lose and your heart broken *so that* you might see the goodness of God, *so that* you might see Christ's compassionate love pointing you in the right direction. Yes, these are the times when—finally—we come to the end of ourselves, and in sheer desperation, cry to God for mercy. And He hears.

BREAKING GROUND

Can you recall a time in your life when everything around you and within you seemed broken, chaotic, and bleak? How did God meet you?

DARK DAYS

Peter's crisis of faith in the courtyard was a point of "coming to the end of himself"—and it was where God wanted him to be all along. Finally, the self-confident disciple was shaken, his resources spent. The sound of the rooster's crowing took Peter to the depths of his own depravity and showed him his utter inability to follow Jesus. By himself he could do nothing, except sin (and he did that pretty well). With God's Holy Spirit breathing new life in him, Peter could become a rock.

Even before Jesus died, Peter had come to this place of absolute despondency and need. Not only was he despairing at the condition of his soul—the first step in any authentic conversion—but he probably lost all hope when he watched his Lord's violent death on a cross outside of town. The gospel writers do not tell us where Peter was when Jesus was tried before Pontius Pilate or when his Friend from Nazareth was beaten, flogged, and ridiculed or when nails were finally driven through His wrists and feet and His cross was hoisted up. During what were undoubtedly the darkest hours the earth has ever known, Peter could have been anywhere. But most likely he was nearby.

We do know that after Jesus' body was laid in a tomb, the broken fisherman from Galilee returned to his friends, a group no doubt experiencing a corporate crisis of faith. Though Christ had warned them time and again that His death was certain, how could they have known it would be this terrible, that their life together would be so horribly threatened?

But as they had seen with their own eyes many, many times, despair and agony could not last long if Jesus was on the scene. When Mary discovered the stone had been rolled away from the mouth of the grave, she reported it to Peter and John. (This in itself is an extraordinary detail for John to include. Why? Because women in those times were marginal citizens and would never have been credited with firsthand reports of such news—unless, of course, they actually *were* the first witnesses.) The slightest possibility set the broken yet passionate apostle in motion, and he ran with all his heart toward the tomb.

Though the other disciple (John) arrived first, Peter was the one who acted boldly: He walked right into the grave—the place where a dead human body should have been stinking and decaying—and stopped in his tracks. There was no stench because there was *no body!* Instead, there were only grave cloths tidily folded, lying in the center of the tomb.

Jesus was alive.

Read John 20:1-9.

FIRST LOOKS

1. How do you think Peter's brokenness—from denying Jesus—prepared him for what he might find at the tomb?

2. Why do you suppose Peter barged right into the burial tomb? What does that say about his personality and his place on his spiritual journey?

3. After his denial of Christ, Peter probably did not expect to see Jesus face to face again, let alone continue in the ministry. What feelings could he have experienced now that he knew Jesus was alive?

4. Do you think Peter expected to be forgiven? Why or why not?

Read John 21:1-23.

MORNING LIGHT

Even knowing Jesus was no longer dead, Peter didn't appear to be convinced of His mandate to build God's church. It's likely Jesus had appeared to the disciples a few times before the wonderful story in John 21, but it is also important to remember that the events in John's gospel were not written in chronological order. That means that the disciples may already have seen the resurrected Lord even before this extraordinary morning, but it does not mean they were any less surprised by what happened.

His confidence understandably shaken, Peter went back to the vocation he knew best: fishing. When he announced this to his friends, they, too, liked the idea—what else did they have to do?—and invited themselves along. Out they went, the sun setting, their hearts restless. And out they stayed until the sun came up the next morning. The joke was on them, they must have thought, because at dawn their nets were still empty.

Sunlight was barely shining on the water when they heard a shout from shore, someone calling to them to cast their net on the other side of the boat. Either the suggestion sounded vaguely familiar, or they figured they had nothing to lose. Or both. But when they tossed their net into the water, they could not even haul it in because it had so many fish! This was more like it; this would get them somewhere.

But something was strange. Hadn't this happened before? Hadn't there been another time when the Man from Nazareth had called to them, when they had made the catch of a lifetime, and He had told them they would become fishers of men? Now, with 153 fish (to be exact!) flopping all over the deck, chaos and shouting filled the boat. One disciple, however, had the presence of mind to look toward the shore, and when he did, he understood why their catch was an abundant one: Jesus was standing there. John pointed and said to Peter, "It is the Lord!" (verse 7). When Peter heard this news from his friend, and without even looking up, he threw on his clothes—lest he appear improper before the Lord—and dived *into* the water, swimming with all his might toward the One he had just denied knowing days before.

There, Jesus greeted him. And there, the Lord of the universe again did the unexpected: He made breakfast for His friends. They were hungry, after all, having spent the night at sea. Surely, though, He could have set up a ministry headquarters or preached a sermon or performed a few more miracles in front of them. Instead, the Savior who had just experienced the most excruciating pain a human—and God—could endure as He hung on the cross, who had spent three days in hell conquering death, was now serving them. Again. Not only had He provided for them another astonishing catch, He was cooking breakfast for them as well, emphasizing to all His followers—then and now—that God provides for His children personally, abundantly, and consistently. No matter what crises they've faced.

Giving to us is His nature.

TAKING IT IN

5. What about Jesus motivated Peter to jump ship and swim to shore? What had happened to make him so driven to see the Man he'd so deeply disappointed?

6. Look at Luke 5:1-11 again. What is the difference between this first catch and the last? How did Peter's response to the first catch differ from the last?

7. John included the number of fish—153—probably for no other reason than that someone actually counted. It is more of a journalistic detail than a theologically significant point. What might this enormous catch symbolize to the disciples about Christ's work and mission in the world?

8. What do you think it would be like to have breakfast with Jesus? What would it look like to you?

THE CALLING BEGINS

Those of us who have walked through agonizing moments of doubt or have avoided doing the right thing know—at least in hindsight—that in spite of how we may feel about those moments, they are not lost. God redeems them. That is, they were part of the journey that taught us again who we are and, more accurately, who we are not. They reminded us, too, just how patient our Maker is, just how gracious our Savior is in loving us, changing us, and using us to build His kingdom in this world. I suspect we will learn and relearn this lesson as long as we remain in these earthly bodies, stuck in a culture where justice and righteousness compete minute by minute with selfishness and greed. God help us.

Known as his "recommissioning," Peter's interaction with Jesus after breakfast is one more remarkable example of how individually unique God is with His children. Three times the fisherman had denied knowing the Christ; now three times Jesus gave the fisherman an opportunity to state otherwise. To do it over, if you will. But more than that, the Lord also understood what His friend was feeling about his purpose. He understood that Peter had reverted to fishing, was second-guessing his calling, and felt distant from the Man who'd first offered him the opportunity to fish for men's souls. Now the broken disciple was ready to receive a new identity.

"Simon son of John," Jesus said to him—the name Jesus had used when they had first met (John 21:15). Why did Jesus use this name again? So that the fisherman would never again forget where he was from—who he had been and not been—and what Christ had brought him through.

It did not change his calling as the rock on which Jesus would build His church, but Peter needed to remember, and then remember again, that he was both greatly sinful and extravagantly loved.

The Lord then looked deep into His follower's heart and took the conversation in an intensely personal direction. Jesus asked Peter if he loved Him. Here, the Greek word for love is *agape,* which is the highest and godliest form of love. And Peter, in utter humility and brokenness, responded by using the Greek word *phileo,* a word for love used mostly between friends. "Yes, Lord, you know that I am your friend," Peter said (see John 21:15-16). Gone was the Peter who bragged to Jesus about never falling away from Him. Gone was the Peter who boasted about going to his death for the Lord. Here, Peter was finally honest in his self-assessment: All he could offer Jesus was his friendship.

Again the Lord asked Peter about agape love, and again Peter responded with phileo friendship (see verse 16). But the third time, Jesus spoke on Peter's level and used *phileo* in His question: "Are you my friend?" It was as if He wanted the apostle to profess his love honestly and sincerely for Jesus as his friend, establishing this as the place from which Peter would receive his "reinstatement" that would eventually lead to the greatest church movement the world has ever known.

With his love now redirected to his Lord as his top priority, Peter was then encouraged to forgo the idea of fishing and instead become a shepherd. Christ's love not only inspired an identity change, but it created a new purpose. "Feed my lambs," "Take care of my sheep," "Feed my sheep," the Lord charged after each of Peter's responses (verses 15-17). Be careful, though, Peter, for in pursuing the call of God, the cost will be great. It always is.

So Peter was forgiven. He was restored. He was loved. Brought back from his crisis of faith and empowered for an entirely new work as a shepherd. Peter, however, could not stop being Peter, even in the excitement of this new revelation. Old habits die hard. As usual, Peter's tongue got the best of him, and he insisted on meddling in business not his own.

"What about him?" he bluntly asked Jesus about what would happen to another disciple (verse 21).

Oh, how easily our eyes roam! I imagine at this point, the Lord grabbed Peter's chin, pulled it back toward His face, and stared hard into those passionate eyes in front of Him. Then He once again offered Peter the greatest adventure he would ever know, one that still echoes to us thousands of years—and crises—later: "Never mind about anyone else. Follow Me" (see verse 22).

And though he could not have known it at the time, Peter's decision to follow Jesus would change history.

Making It Real

9. Christ dealt with Peter in a way that was unique to Peter's crisis of faith—by offering him three opportunities to profess his new faith. In what ways has God uniquely responded to you and led you in a new direction?

10. Jesus pursued Peter so he could fulfill what he'd been created to do: build God's church. What does this reveal to you about the character of Jesus? about His invitation to us to participate in His work?

11. What do Christ's words "Follow Me" mean to you today?

Much of the Christian life is about asking for and receiving forgiveness from God for the times we fall short of His best for our lives. Revel in that forgiveness now. Ask Him for grace to keep your eyes on Him as you enjoy the adventure of life with Him.

> The fact is that the same moment which brings the consciousness of having sinned, ought to bring also the consciousness of being forgiven. This is especially essential to an unwavering walk in the highway of holiness, for no separation from God can be tolerated here for an instant.
>
> We can only walk in this path by looking continually unto Jesus, moment by moment, and if our eyes are taken off of Him to look upon our own sin and our own weakness, we shall leave the path at once. The believer, therefore, who has, as he trusts, entered upon this highway, if he finds himself overcome by sin must flee with it instantly to Jesus. He must act on 1 John 1:9, "If we confess our sins, he is faithful and just to forgive us our sins, and to cleanse us from all unrighteousness." He must not hide his sin and seek to salve it over with excuses, or to push it out of his memory by the lapse of time. But he must do as the children of Israel did, rise up "early in the morning," and "run" to the place where the evil thing is hidden, and take it out of its hiding place, and lay it "out before the Lord." He must confess his sin.
>
> —HANNAH WHITALL SMITH, *The Christian's Secret of a Happy Life*

SIX

REAL POWER: LEADING
BY EXAMPLE

ACTS 1–4

*Ever since the spider had befriended him, he had done his
best to live up to his reputation. When Charlotte's web said
SOME PIG, Wilbur had tried to look like some pig. When
Charlotte's web said TERRIFIC, Wilbur had tried to look
terrific. And now that the web said RADIANT, he did
everything possible to make himself glow.*

—E. B. WHITE, *Charlotte's Web*

Lynn was a champion gymnast when we were in high school together. I
loved going to her meets and watching her bend, throw, and turn her
body around in ways I never thought humanly possible. She'd mount the
balance beam into a handstand, point her legs straight above her like an
arrow, and then swing them down onto the beam where she'd do the
splits—and this was just the start of her routine! Or she'd bounce her waist
hard against the uneven bars and propel herself from the force to the
higher bar, then the lower bar, then back again. Or she'd run down the
floor at locomotive speed, jump onto a little springboard, grip her hands

on a vault, and fly through the air in a series of twists and somersaults before landing with both feet perfectly planted on the mat. As someone who sat on the bench during my own basketball games, I marveled at Lynn's athletic ability.

But Lynn's ease and finesse in the gym did not seem to carry over into other areas of her life. She fell hard for a guy a few years her senior who demanded much and gave back very little. She battled to keep her weight down for gymnastics by binging and purging every now and then, or she would try to numb her pain by going to party after party. Though she was confident enough to fly over vaults, there was little else Lynn felt secure about.

When we graduated, I attended a teachers college, and Lynn earned a gymnastics scholarship for one of the state's best university programs about forty miles away. She followed her abusive boyfriend there, and to control her weight, her coach put her on a diet of one egg and a piece of cheese a day. She spent her days either in class or at the gym and her nights trying to cope with a young man who had no sense of how to care for a woman. Lynn was miserable.

One night my gymnast friend surprised me and appeared at my dorm room. She knew something needed to change in her life, and she wondered if I could help. Me? The benchwarmer? I was worried about Lynn and didn't know what to offer her. Then she asked me about Jesus, and that led us into a conversation that lasted throughout the night, though I think I mumbled through most of it. When Lynn got into her car the next morning and drove back to the university, I didn't know if any of her questions had found answers. In fact, I wondered what would happen to her.

The next year, though, Lynn decided to give up her scholarship, her boyfriend, and her misery. She called to tell me she was transferring to my college and wondered if she could be my roommate. "Oh, and I decided to follow Jesus," she said to me with a seriousness that both startled and delighted me. Not only was her faith commitment sincere, but she spent the next few years devouring the Bible and enjoying the fellowship she found at a local church. As I watched the changes in her life, I marveled once again at my friend.

Today, Lynn—along with her husband and six children—runs a fantastic ministry for single mothers in Suva, Fiji.⁷ She teaches parenting classes, leads Bible studies, builds friendships with women in tough situations, and laughs at almost every joke imaginable. In fact, she's known for her laughter. The joy Lynn discovered—and continues to discover—in the person of Jesus Christ transformed every part of her life, giving her a security that she wouldn't trade for all the championships in the world.

BREAKING GROUND

In what ways have you watched someone's life transformed when she or he encountered the truth of Jesus Christ?

DEEP BREATHS

Oh, the power and drama of conversion. There is nothing quite like watching a fellow human respond to the grace and goodness of the Maker of the universe, seeing his or her weaknesses turned into strengths, fears transformed into faith, and the contagious effect this has on others. So it is particularly moving, in light of all the times we watched Peter fall on his face—literally or not—to see him move from whining follower to an emerging leader and holy apostle. In fact, when I read through the first four chapters of Acts, when I watch Peter's humble leadership, listen to his voice, and observe his confidence and faith, I wonder if this is the same Galilean fisherman we met in the gospel accounts. I cannot help but ask, "Who *is* this guy?!"

Why, of course it was Peter, the man Christ kept calling forth, the rock at which He kept chiseling. It was the leader Jesus poured Himself into, the sinner He died for. And it was the brother whom God's Holy Spirit breathed on, the shepherd who went on to care for his friends. All of these things describe the man we know as Peter the apostle.

The details of his transformed life are astounding. In the first chapter of Acts, after he listened again to the words of his resurrected Lord (see verses 4-8) and watched Him ascend into heaven, Peter returned with his friends to Jerusalem and took charge—in a humbled way, that is. He appealed to their biblical memory by quoting Scripture and put a suggestion on the table for them to consider: Now that Judas was, um, gone, they needed to replace him.

Peter was certainly aware that his own denial of Christ was as troubling as Judas's betrayal. However, for purposes only God could know, Peter had been spared the fate of his former colleague, and now he had the opportunity to do what he had personally promised Jesus: follow Him. At this point that meant their gathering of followers needed another first-hand witness to continue the work they'd be given, so Peter led them through the process of prayer and selection.

Then, in the greatest event since the Resurrection itself—the Day of Pentecost—Peter was given the most prominent role he'd had yet. As God's presence became apparent (certainly, by now Peter must have been getting used to the unexpected), he and his friends were filled with the Holy Spirit, and once again, they did something they'd never done before: They began to speak in other tongues or languages.

A crowd gathered. Neighbors were confounded. International visitors suddenly heard these Galileans speaking in their own native tongues. Rumors spread. Chaos built.

And Peter—the man who wouldn't tell even a few people around a fire that he had known Jesus—now stood up, raised his voice, and began to address the diverse audience. He recalled the words of the Hebrew prophets, the relentless plan of God to draw men to Himself, and the hope of calling on Him to be saved. Then he addressed the times in which they lived and talked about a subject with which he was intimately familiar: Jesus of Nazareth. The Man who performed miracles and wonders. The Man Peter's audience had handed over to wicked men. The Man they had put to death on the cross, but the Man whom God had raised again, "because it was impossible for death to keep its hold on him" (Acts 2:24).

When the crowd heard his words, they "were cut to the heart" (2:37) and asked him what they should do. The broken but filled fisherman-turned-shepherd answered them with—what else?—boldness and passion: "Repent and be baptized, every one of you, in the name of Jesus Christ for the forgiveness of your sins. And you will receive the gift of the Holy Spirit. The promise is for you and your children and for all who are far off—for all whom the Lord our God will call" (2:38-39).

What? The man who once rebuked his Lord for daring to wash his feet now was encouraging absolute strangers to call on Jesus and get clean! Peter's life *had* indeed changed, and everyone around him was affected by it.

Read Acts 1 and 2.

First Looks

1. What leadership qualities do you see in Peter?

2. Why do you think the Holy Spirit fell on the church with tongues of other languages? What does that suggest about God's heart for cultural diversity?

3. How did the crowd respond to Peter's message? How did the church—the gathering of believers—respond?

4. What distinguished the "fellowship of the believers" in 2:42-47?

Read Acts 3.

THE DRAMA CONTINUES

The third and fourth chapters of Acts read a bit like a screenplay. Miracles. Drama. Action. Adventure. In each scene the stakes were raised for our hero, and the more we read, the more we wonder what could happen next.

Thankfully, though, Peter's encounters after Pentecost were the stuff of real life, not Hollywood, of a real God, not a special-effects editor. Yes,

Peter had fallen from his Savior, but now his faith had been restored and seemed to grow from a tiny mustard seed into a full-size tree. At this point Peter was more than confident of what God could do. He had personally experienced Almighty Power.

As Peter and John walked toward the temple to pray, a crippled man greeted them and asked for some spare change. Beggars often stood outside the holy places, hoping for a little supernatural compassion to come their way. This situation was no different. But these apostles were not ordinary religious men. They had been with Jesus. One in particular had experienced the extraordinary freedom of forgiveness, the gift of another chance. The beggar obviously had no idea just whom he was dealing with.

When Peter heard the request from the poor man, he knew what he had to do. He offered the riches of Christ in exchange for the beggar's poverty of soul. Peter, the man who before had relied too much on his own ingenuity in crisis moments, now pointed upward, experiencing a Power more real—and certainly more humbling—than he had imagined. And just as his Lord had shown him many times before, Peter wasn't interested in giving someone temporary relief from pain; he offered instead the healing that comes simply at the name of Jesus.

I will be the first to confess that too many times I have believed I had little to give to people in need. Sometimes when a person asking for money has approached me on the street, I've shaken my head and kept walking. Sometimes I've pulled out a dollar. But rarely have I sensed the spiritual courage or nudging to reach out my hand, look into the person's eyes and say—like Peter did—"I don't have any money, but I'll give you what I have. Here, meet Jesus." I wonder how different our lives—and our world—would be if we began to take such action in faith!

Peter's bold profession of faith, of course, had not developed overnight. It was a process of growing with Jesus. Nor did it happen without consequences, for as the now walking—and jumping and praising—beggar held on to Peter and John, a crowd gathered, and some religious leaders were not happy (see verse 11 and Acts 4:2). Still, the people could hardly believe their eyes. And the daring apostle saw the opportunity to again point his audience to his Lord. In fact, he told it plainly: "By faith in the name of Jesus, this man whom you see and know was made strong. It is Jesus' name and the faith that comes through him that has given this complete healing to him, as you can all see" (Acts 3:16).

Simple faith. A powerful Name. Dramatic change.

TAKING IT IN

5. Why do you think the lame man was willing to let Peter help him?

6. Notice that the beggar's response to his healing was to praise God. How did the crowd react when they saw him? What impact might the man's testimony have had on them (verses 9-11)?

7. What does Peter's speech (verses 12-26) reveal about the changes in his character? What still sounds familiar?

Read Acts 4.

IRRATIONAL FAITH

Peter's boldness not only attracted the attention of many people hungry for the truth of the gospel, but it provided him with an opportunity to preach. But make no mistake: It also upset the local religious leaders. In fact, verses 1-7 suggest his words and actions were so disturbing, so threatening to the status quo, that our hero was arrested and thrown into jail. Peter was no doubt beginning to understand the cost of his obedience. Nonetheless, the word was out, and "many who heard the message believed, and the number of men grew to about five thousand" (verse 4).

When Peter was brought before the religious leaders the next day to defend himself, the old doubting, impulsive fisherman was nowhere to be found. The new Peter, filled with a Spirit not his own, spoke before the council, proclaiming the message of Christ's power to heal. Peter even went so far as to tell the Jewish leaders, the powerful governing teachers of the town who clung to Hebrew traditions, that "salvation is found in no one else, for there is no other name under heaven given to men by which we must be saved" (verse 12).

This declaration presented a serious problem to the intellectuals of the day—as it can in our day as well. For one thing, the leaders did not understand how such "unschooled, ordinary" men as Peter and John could have acquired these spiritual insights (verse 13). And they certainly could not deny that the apostles had performed a most astonishing miracle—the healed beggar was, after all, standing beside them for everyone in Jerusalem to see. Even more troubling was the idea that salvation could only be found through a Man who died an excruciating death at the hands of evil men and who somehow came alive again a few days later. None of it was rational; none of it made sense. This declaration provoked one of two responses: faith or denial.

And if Peter was going to have anything to say about it, he would say it! He challenged the traditional thinking of these Hebrew leaders. They responded by ordering Peter and John "not to speak or teach at all in the name of Jesus" (verse 18). Peter, however, could not contain himself or his passion; neither could his friend John. Their defense stumped the leaders: "Judge for yourselves whether it is right in God's sight to obey you rather than God. For we cannot help speaking about what we have seen and heard" (verse 19).

Peter's passion was redeemed for God's purposes as he professed that, well, he just could not help himself! He'd been with God! He'd been forgiven! He'd been loved and encouraged and changed. How could he *not* speak?! Yes, his radical conversion was yielding a radical lifestyle, one that challenged everyone around him and encouraged many to believe. It was a lifestyle that also encouraged his fellow believers to participate in one of the most radical examples of Christian love the world had known—before or since.

Finally, Peter had gotten it right. Or rather, the Righteous One had "gotten" him.

MAKING IT REAL

8. Peter's "act of kindness to a cripple" landed him in jail. Why do you think the local religious leaders were so threatened by him? Why are people still threatened by the message Peter proclaimed?

9. At what times in your life have you not been able to help "speaking about what [you] have seen and heard" (verse 20)?

10. When Peter and John returned to their friends after being imprisoned, what did the disciples tell them? How did the believers respond? What does their response say about community?

11. In what ways does Peter's boldness with the beggar challenge you in responding to the needs of the people around you?

12. Consider the amazing description in verses 32-35 of the believers' community that Peter was a part of as well as their witness to the world. Also look back on 2:42-47. What aspects of this picture of the early church are relevant for contemporary followers of Christ? Ask God to move in you and your church in ways that reflect this early example of Christian love.

I remember coming home from a meeting in Brooklyn many years ago, sitting in an uncomfortable bus seat facing a few poor people. One of them, a downcast, ragged man, suddenly epitomized for me the desolation, the hopelessness of the destitute, and I began to weep. I had been struck by one of those beams of love, wounded by it in a most particular way. It was my own condition that I was weeping about—my own hardness of heart, my own sinfulness.... Take away my heart of stone and give me a heart of flesh, so that I may learn how to truly love my brother because in him, in his meanest guise, I am encountering Christ.

—DOROTHY DAY, *By Little and by Little*

SEVEN

CONVERTED—AGAIN: MIRACLES OF CHANGE

ACTS 9:32-43; 10

"Hear this, Mundo Cani Dog," he said. His voice was like sand. He put two wings on either side of the Dog's great nose. "If it is God's curse which a Dog brought with him into this Coop, then a Rooster needs the curse of God. Can you believe this? If it were a bushel of fleas which a Dog brought with him, then this Rooster would be happy for a bushel of fleas. A Rooster needs a Dog. A Rooster has come to love him. Stay."

—WALTER WANGERIN, JR., *The Book of the Dun Cow*

Miracles should not happen. A car in Vermont swerves across three lanes of wintry highway without hitting another car, crashes into a guardrail without flipping over, and, save a few emotional bruises, the driver and the passenger breathe normally as they walk away. Alive when they shouldn't be.

A doctor in Colorado tells a young mother that her child is in a coma—measles gone awry—and this will probably be the little girl's last night. The child, though, wakes up three days later wondering why she's in such a stuffy room that stinks like medicine. Healthy when she shouldn't be.

A group of strangers in New York City—black, Latino, white—gathers on a Saturday morning to unload boxes from a U-Haul truck that's just arrived from Mississippi. They carry in the chairs, plants, lamps, and books for the woman they've never before met who is moving into an apartment next door. Included when she shouldn't be.

My *Oxford English Dictionary* helps me understand what is not understandable: "Miracle—a marvelous event exceeding the known powers of nature and therefore supposed to be due to the special intervention of the Deity or of some supernatural agency; an act exhibiting control over the laws of nature and serving as evidence that the agent is either divine or is specially favored by God; a wonderful object, a marvel, a legend."

Snowflakes on my forehead never felt better than that marvelous January day my friend and I climbed out of our smashed-up car. My mother always believed it was divine intervention that woke me up from a coma and put life back into my little soul. And to this day I feel "specially favored by God" when I remember the dozens of people I didn't even know who gave up their Saturday morning to welcome me to their neighborhood. They were members of the church I'd be attending. They were Christians.

These experiences have helped me see that miracles don't fit neatly into a person's framework. They cannot be reduced to the theological constructs that comprise only a few religious traditions nor can they be categorized on a hierarchy of greatness, as if one miracle is better than another. Nor can they be identified merely as showpieces of old-time revivals and healing services. Because if they do indeed "exceed the known powers of nature," then an act of "legend" proportions can occur any minute of the day, any place along the journey, serving as evidence that the One who was and is and is to come never stops acting on our behalf. He just asks us to keep our eyes open.

BREAKING GROUND

How would you define *miracle?* What miracles have you encountered in your life?

EVERYDAY MIRACLES

Miracles should not have happened for the apostle Peter—that impulsive, wishy-washy fisherman from Galilee who was hardly able to stand up on his own, let alone command manna to rain down from heaven or waters to part. But miracles did happen for Peter because miracles are never about a person's ability. They are about God's power and purposes. In fact, as his ministry and leadership in the early church grew, Peter became accustomed to miracles—that is, if one can ever become accustomed to miracles. Can the divinely impossible ever seem humanly possible? Can the unnatural movements of God ever seem natural to mere mortals like us? Can they ever become common? Or routine?

Empowered with the Holy Breath of God, Peter traveled the countryside to fulfill his Lord's command to "feed my sheep" (John 21:17). He watched the Almighty perform some extraordinary deeds to confirm his work in building the church. In Acts 9:32-35, Peter came across a familiar situation: He encountered a paralyzed man. The man's chronic condition had left him bedridden for eight years, but this didn't intimidate Peter. Nor did it seem to elicit any sympathy from him. If anything, because Peter was seeing through different eyes, eyes expecting the unexpected, he looked at the man and wanted only one thing for him: healing.

So Peter spoke these words: "Jesus Christ heals you. Get up and take care of your mat" (verse 34). Like Jesus', Peter's word was as good as his deed, for the man immediately rose to his feet. As if that weren't miracle enough, when *all* those who lived in the town saw the paralyzed man *standing* before them, they, too, turned their hearts to God.

Peter was living out the reality that God's ability defies natural law.

Read Acts 9:32-43.

FIRST LOOKS

1. After reading about Pentecost in Acts 2, we read in Acts 5–8 about the many extraordinary events that Peter was involved in: Scores of sick people were healed under Peter's shadow (see 5:15); jailed again, Peter watched an angel of the Lord open the door and release him (see 5:19); he preached non-stop of the "good news that Jesus is the Christ" (5:42); and he prayed countless times for believers to receive the Holy Spirit (see 8:14-17). How do you think experiences of seeing God's work built Peter's faith and prepared him for this encounter with Aeneas?

2. What was the first thing Peter told Aeneas? What does this say about Peter's confidence?

3. What did Peter tell Aeneas to do (verse 34)? What did this require of Aeneas?

4. Why would the miracle of Aeneas's healing encourage the townspeople to believe in God (verse 35)?

FAMILY RESEMBLANCE

Shortly after his interaction with Aeneas, Peter received urgent word from his friends in a nearby town asking him to come as quickly as possible (see verse 38). Another passionate disciple had taken ill there, a woman who was "always doing good and helping the poor" (verse 36). But before Peter could arrive, the generous sister had lost her fight with the sickness, and death had come quickly. Her heart stopped beating, her lungs stopped breathing, her organs stopped functioning. Her life was gone. And so her friends did what any friends would do at such a time: They began preparing her for burial by washing her lifeless body and placing it in an out-of-the-way room. And they wept at the loss of their friend.

Peter probably heard their laments even before he entered the house. When he stood among them inside, they did another normal thing. In between sobs they pulled out reminders of the woman they had called

Tabitha, robes she'd sewn for them, clothing she'd patched together (see verse 39). Remnants of a friend they dearly loved, tangible memories of a woman whose influence they clearly felt. Grief was heavy in the house, and Peter sensed it too.

Typical of his character, Peter's response was completely unpredictable. First, at the risk of appearing offensive or insensitive—though neither had obviously stopped him before—the apostle asked Tabitha's friends to leave the room. He cleared out the well-meaning group and stood alone with the corpse of this friend. But this was, after all, the same man who had chatted with Jesus *after* he'd watched Him die, who had felt the Lord's normal stomach and hands *after* he had seen them pierced, who had listened carefully to His voice *after* he had heard His final scream on the cross. Peter was familiar with death, and these days he was familiar with resurrection. In fact, this ordinary disciple knew—like the apostle Paul would someday—that the same power that raised Christ from the dead was now at work in him.

Peter dropped to his knees. He turned his eyes heavenward. And he prayed. Earnestly, passionately. No doubt he argued again with God, demanding as usual that the Almighty consider his assessment of the situation. And no doubt he reminded God of the time he had watched Jesus breathe life back into a child, or the time he had heard his Lord call forth from the tomb an already dead friend named Lazarus.

Whatever occurred during his conversation with the Giver of all good gifts, Peter felt certain enough to turn toward the dead woman lying a few feet from him and tell her simply to get up. It was not an emotional plea or a grief-stricken appeal, nor was it full of uncertainty or despair. No, Peter's instruction was bold and clear—and transcendent—as he called the woman out of darkness and back into the light of life. She opened her eyes, saw the scraggly fisherman still on his knees, and sat up (see verse 40).

Naturally, Peter then presented Tabitha to her friends again; she was breathing, walking, and ready to sew some more robes.

Taking It In

5. Peter did more than interact with Tabitha in words. When Peter saw Tabitha sit up, what did he do (verse 41)? What does his action remind you of?

6. How do you suppose the woman's friends responded when they saw her alive again?

7. The Bible says that this event became known all over town, and "many people believed in the Lord" (verse 42). What about this event might have persuaded skeptics to believe?

Read Acts 10.

A Change of Heart—Again

As phenomenal as it would be to watch a paralyzed man regain the use of his legs or to see a dead woman suddenly alive again, it is important to remember that God's abilities are not limited to changing a person's physical condition. Changing someone's heart is a miracle of its own, one that invites praise to the King of glory. Though someone might have encountered or experienced various miracles firsthand, they do not make him or her a spiritual giant or incapable of sin. We must not forget that miracles are about God's ability, not man's, and that the process of conversion is just that: a process that even the most gifted leaders of the faith continue to go through. Instant miracles do not keep us from being human.

Which leads us back, of course, to the passionate—and human—apostle Peter. Yes, God's favor had rested on this Jewish fisherman in ways he never could have imagined. He had lived with Jesus for three years. He had been empowered by God's Spirit at Pentecost. He had preached the resurrecting hope of Christ to crowds of hungry souls. His own hands had healed the sick and raised the dead. But Peter was, well, still Peter, and that meant he was still susceptible to getting it wrong. Though he was certainly a radical follower of Christ and a powerful leader of God's church, Peter—like all of us—was not immune to the dangers of sin.

Shortly after he held Tabitha's warm hand and watched her walk back into the fellowship of their friends, Peter experienced another unexpected turn on his journey. He'd been staying in the same town where Tabitha lived, died, and lived again. One day he needed a solitary place to pray, so he went up on the roof (see verse 9). Instead of praying, though, he fell into a trance and had a vision of four-footed animals being lowered out of heaven on a sheet (see verse 12). When a Voice in the dream told him to "kill and eat" (verse 13), the old obstinate, self-righteous Peter surfaced, the one who had argued with God.

"'Surely not, Lord!' Peter replied. 'I have never eaten anything impure or unclean'" (verse 15). But God was preparing him for something he did not see coming, and the Voice commanded Peter not to call anything impure or unclean that God had made clean. It took three times for Peter to hear correctly (see verse 16), but eventually it sunk in, though he still did not understand what it meant.

These must surely have been strange words for a religious leader like Peter to hear. After all, he was steeped in Jewish tradition that forbade even the eating of particular foods. It was one thing for Peter to be confident of the power of his Messiah, but quite another to look beyond the comforting and familiar territory of his Jewish identity. This strange vision God had sent just did not make sense; how could He ask Peter to go outside the customs of His chosen culture? Weren't Jewish traditions the right traditions? Weren't they supreme and therefore better than any others? Peter was perplexed. By modern terms, Peter was ethnocentric. Some might even call him a bigot, albeit a well-meaning one.

But the God whom he professed to serve was not partial to one group of people over another. In fact, He was orchestrating another miracle by introducing the stubborn Jew to a righteous Gentile man named Cornelius, a man whom God would use to chisel away another piece of the apostle's heart. And when Peter, against his better Jewish judgment, entered Cornelius's home, his heart was pierced, and the miracle of another sort took place, what I like to call Peter's "race conversion." The ethnocentric lens through which he had viewed the world lifted, and Peter proclaimed to his new non-Jewish friends, "I now realize how true it is that God does not show favoritism but accepts men from every nation who fear him and do what is right. You know the message God sent to the people of Israel, telling the good news of peace through Jesus Christ, who is Lord of all" (verses 34-36).

Peter's cross-cultural repentance provided him an amazing opportunity to reach people he would not have thought about had God not intentionally directed him to them. They in turn responded to the good news as the Holy Spirit came upon them as well (see verses 44-46). But as is true of human nature (and history confirms it in every culture and time period), such efforts with "outsiders" come with great human challenges and costs. Acts 11 shows Peter having to explain and defend his interactions with Cornelius to his Jewish friends. Eventually, they accepted his words, but the struggle was obvious. Why? Because celebrating the God-designed diversity of other ethnic groups is often difficult. The rewards though—as Peter experienced—outweigh the challenges.

In fact, when people from different backgrounds come together for the sake of the gospel, it is nothing short of an act of God. It is a miracle from heaven.

MAKING IT REAL

8. Peter was certainly a mighty instrument whom God used to perform miracles. Yet he still needed to grow in a number of areas. What does this suggest about those in church leadership roles? What can you do to best support your church leaders?

9. What type of person was Cornelius? Why would Peter have resisted the idea of going to visit him (verse 28)? What does this suggest about the nature of prejudice?

✐ 10. How does this interaction between Jew and Gentile speak to
       contemporary Christians from all backgrounds? What does the
       fact that God poured out His Holy Spirit on the Gentiles reveal
       about His desire for reconciliation?

11. In what ways could you be intentional about confronting racial
    or ethnic divisions? In what ways have you struggled with these
    issues?

12. What do Peter's encounters with Aeneas, Tabitha, and Cornelius
    reveal to you about God's character and desires for His children?

Ask God to search your heart and show you places where miracles may be
waiting to happen near you—miracles of healing, new life, and unity.

At the center of the Christian faith is the conviction that in the universe there is a God of power who is able to do exceedingly abundant things in nature and in history. This conviction is stressed over and over in the Old and the New Testaments. Theologically, this affirmation is expressed in the doctrine of the omnipotence of God. The God whom we worship is not a weak and incompetent God. He is able to beat back gigantic waves of opposition and to bring low prodigious mountains of evil. The ringing testimony of the Christian faith is that God is able.

—DR. MARTIN LUTHER KING JR., *The Strength to Love*

EIGHT

INSPIRED TO LEAD: PETER WRITES HOME

1 PETER

"Is that the end of the story?" asked Christopher Robin.

"That's the end of that one. There are others."

"About Pooh and Me?"

"And Piglet and Rabbit and all of you. Don't you remember?"…

"I do remember," he said, "only Pooh doesn't very well, so that's why he likes having it told to him again. Because then it's a real story and not just a remembering."

—A. A. MILNE, *Winnie the Pooh*

Last week, one of my favorite things in all the world happened: I received a real, handwritten letter in the mail. Better still, it was from my nine-year-old niece, Karli.

"Dear Aunt Jo," it began in big loopy letters on Big Chief paper. "How are you? I like the book I'm reading. We are working hard in school. My dad went to a conference and I'm playing the piano. Have you gone for any bike rides lately? I have. Love Karli." Though it wasn't a particularly long letter, it was full of nine-year-old life and news and affection, especially the big green letters Karli had formed at the end: "WRITE BACK!"

When I read her letter, it wasn't difficult for me to envision this child frozen on the couch, her brow bent from concentrating on the book plopped across her lap. I imagined her at her desk multiplying fives on her math worksheet or practicing *l*'s and *r*'s in her new cursive handwriting. I "listened" to the variety of notes she found on the upright piano that sits in her family's living room. And I watched her sandy-colored ponytail bob up and down as she rode her Stingray bike down the street. Then, because there is something inviting about a letter, I got out my stationery and wrote back to my niece.

Even without providing much detail, my niece had told me stories in her letter, reflections of what was important to her at this time in her life. They connected me to her when I could not be with her, and they helped me share in her life though I live eight hundred miles away. That's what letters do; they link human souls and feed a bond that otherwise might be lost to time or distance.

But I have to admit: Letter writing can often seem more like an activity from another century—like dipping feathers in inkwells—than a modern mode of communication. In a world of e-mails, Palm Pilots, and cell phones, it is not easy to sit down and write. In fact, it can seem like a time-consuming burden: Pen in hand. Forming sentences on paper rather than a keyboard. No delete button. No simple way to cut and paste ideas. Honestly, it sometimes feels easier just to pick up a phone or write a one-phrase e-mail that can be sent in an instant.

Which, I suppose, is why we appreciate receiving a letter from a friend in the mail, a letter replete with personal stories, encouraging reminders, and interesting insights. A letter we know the writer spent valuable time creating, simply because he or she was thinking of us.

Breaking Ground

Recall a time when you either wrote a particularly meaningful letter or received one from someone who was especially important to you. What was the experience like? Who could you write a letter to right now? (Why not pull out a piece of paper and get it started?)

Peter's Pen

One of the things I love about the Bible is that when the Great Editor was gathering material for His Holy Book, He saw fit to include many personal letters written by the apostles. Real letters with honest words revealing to us the human stuff of discipleship, the spiritual challenges of relationships, and the rewards of staying the course. The New Testament Epistles are certainly inspired, full of life and news and affection, reflecting the issues and priorities that leaders like Peter recognized as important in their time. And like all good writing, they speak across history and cultures to communicate a message that is equally transcendent: God, the Living Word, invites relationship.

Peter's first letter is full of the themes from the three years he spent with Jesus. Now that we "know" Peter a little better from watching him interact with the Lord in the Gospels and with fellow believers and religious leaders in Acts, it is fascinating to read one of his personal letters. The very issues that shaped his character jump off the pages of these five chapters. In 1 Peter, we discover new dimensions of the fisherman-turned-shepherd. In fact, the old belligerent, impetuous Peter is nowhere to be found on these pages. Instead, we see the authority of Peter's leadership within the church and the lessons he learned on the missionary trips he took from Jerusalem to the region we now call the Middle East. In this affectionate and revealing letter, we see a redeemed Peter, and we see how the familiar challenges he confronted were redeemed as well.

There is some disagreement among Bible scholars as to whether Peter actually wrote the letter. Some people suggest the Greek writing was too intellectual for an untrained fisherman from Galilee—similar to the argument of the religious leaders of Peter's day who were astonished to learn that Peter and John were "unschooled, ordinary men" and "took note that these men had been with Jesus" (Acts 4:13). Other scholars claim that it is certainly Peter's voice, pointing to the consistency between the letter and his sermons in Acts, even though the actual handwriting might not have been his. (Some say that Silas wrote for him.)

Whether the apostle used his own hand or that of a scribe to pen the ideas in the letter, the point is that the letter is uniquely Peter's in the same way Karli's letter was uniquely hers. It reflects the issues that were important to him because he experienced them firsthand. And in my opinion, this adds even more credibility to the letter because it reminds us of how God's redemptive plans often surpass man's understanding. For instance, we are not surprised that the key theme in the letter is suffering—a word found over fifteen times in the five chapters—since we know how familiar Peter had been with suffering, both when he watched Jesus beaten and murdered and when he himself was persecuted for his faith after Pentecost. Peter personally experienced how God used such struggles to refine his own faith. Naturally, then, he encouraged his friends to endure current afflictions, "so that your faith—of greater worth than gold, which perishes even though refined by fire—may be proved genuine and may result in praise, glory and honor when Jesus Christ is revealed" (1 Peter 1:7).

Likewise, when we recall the tension Peter felt regarding his Jewish traditions and those of the Gentiles, even the rebuke he received from the apostle Paul for his hypocrisy (see Galatians 2:11-14), we appreciate all the more the ethnically mixed audience Peter addressed at the beginning of his letter: "To God's elect, strangers in the world, scattered throughout Pontus, Galatia, Cappadocia, Asia and Bithynia" (1 Peter 1:1). From his encounter with Cornelius, Peter had learned not to put much trust in the customs of his own culture. By now he knew that all the religious traditions in the world could not bring about salvation. Only a Person could—and did: "For you know that it was not with perishable things such as silver or gold that you were redeemed from the empty way of life handed down to you from your forefathers, but with the precious blood of Christ, a lamb without blemish or defect" (1:18,19). How much more meaningful was his instruction to "above all, love each other deeply, because love covers over a multitude of sins" (4:8).

The same man we once knew as impulsive and unable to control his temper now admonished his friends to be self-controlled (see 1:13 and 4:7). The fisherman who took his eyes off Jesus after he climbed out of a boat and onto a lake now encouraged his readers to "set your hope fully on the grace to be given you when Jesus Christ is revealed" (1:13). The man who argued with the Lord over whether He should die or not, who stumbled from the truth when he denied knowing Christ in the courtyard, now was convinced that Jesus was "chosen before the creation of the world, but was revealed in these last times for your sake. Through him you believe in God, who raised him from the dead and glorified him, and so your faith and hope are in God" (1:20,21). And the one who wavered in his faith now called God's people to "be holy in all you do" (1:15).

Read 1 Peter.

FIRST LOOKS

1. What aspects of Peter's character (or personality) reflect the points he made in his letter?

2. Review Galatians 2:11-14. What was Paul's challenge to Peter, and what insight into Peter does it offer?

3. How would you define *suffering?* In what ways does Peter's letter help you better understand suffering?

4. Notice how much Peter quoted the Hebrew Scriptures. Why do you think he did this? What does it say about him to the readers of his letter?

WRITING HOME

When Peter was on the Mount of Transfiguration, he did not seem to have any idea what real authority looked like. Now in this letter he wrote about—of all things!—what it means to submit "for the Lord's sake to every authority instituted among men" (2:13). What welcome words these must have been to those who knew Peter when issues like authority and self-control had been foreign concepts to him. Certainly, his life now reflected the miraculous—and patient—work of the Almighty. Over the years God had indeed lifted the delusions Peter had created about himself, helping him grow into the person God intended him to be. No wonder Peter could tell others to "rid yourselves of all malice and all deceit, hypocrisy, envy, and slander of every kind. Like newborn babies, crave pure spiritual milk, so that by it you may grow up in your salvation, now that you have tasted that the Lord is good" (2:1-3). If anyone had grown up and tasted God's goodness, Peter had!

He could also write about being "chosen" (2:9) because he had heard Jesus calling to him from shore and inviting him to "follow me" (Mark 1:17). He could write about being called "out of darkness" (2:9) because after he himself had experienced the Light of Life—Jesus resurrected—he had knelt beside a dead woman to call her out of the darkness of death and back into life.

Obviously, Peter's letter reveals a profound identity shift, a radical change of understanding about who he was and who he was not. Life with Jesus had forever transformed the apostle, and now he could not help but remind others that "to this you were called, because Christ suffered for you, leaving you an example, that you should follow in his steps" (2:21). Though Peter had often reacted by *not* following in Jesus' steps—by drawing a sword in the garden, for example—he also knew from standing beside Him that Christ did not react to suffering as we would. Peter knew firsthand that Jesus was different from any other man in all of history, that He "did not retaliate; when he suffered, he made no threats. Instead, he entrusted himself to him who judges justly" (2:23).

Yes, Christ had been his example. But Peter knew that the Carpenter from Nazareth was much more than that: "He himself bore our sins in his body on the tree, so that we might die to sins and live for righteousness; by his wounds you have been healed" (2:24). Peter's sins had been carried in the body of his Lord, and as a result, *his* wounds had been healed. Now he could live for righteousness! And how much he identified with the reality of his own words: "For you were like sheep going astray, but now you have returned to the Shepherd and Overseer of your souls" (2:25). Peter had walked, eaten, lived with—and strayed from—the One whose entire purpose in coming to the earth was to redeem imperfect humans like him! Consequently, Peter was a completely new man.

In fact, Peter was now keenly aware of how he would fulfill the mission Jesus had given him. Only by obeying "the stone the builders rejected...a stone that causes men to stumble and a rock that makes them fall" (2:7,8) could the "rock" on whom Christ would build His church be effective. Only by directing others to "be shepherds of God's flock" (5:2) and turning their attention to the Chief Shepherd who would appear again (see 5:4) could Peter do what Jesus had asked of him at his recommissioning: Feed My sheep.

In other words, Christ the Rock was now Peter's only hope of being a rock, and Christ the Great Shepherd was Peter's only hope of shepherding others. His identity and mission as rock and shepherd were inextricably linked with Jesus, the Lamb who was slain and who lived again, the One who was and is and is to come.

Certainly, that was news worth writing his friends about.

Taking It In

5. How is Peter's shift in understanding authority and submission relevant to contemporary Christians living in a culture with varying views of both?

6. What verses in his letter reveal Peter's new sense of identity and mission?

7. Peter's letter reveals a very clear picture of who Jesus is. What words did he use to paint that picture? What adjectives or nouns did Peter use to describe Jesus?

CARRYING THE NEWS

One of the most remarkable verses in Peter's entire letter is located smack in the middle of the chapters. Some might say it's buried under all his other famous points about suffering, and can be easy to miss. But that does not diminish its importance. In fact, it is a verse on which modern defenders of the Christian faith base much of their apologetics.

I can see why. For here in the heart of his letter, one of history's most famous "failures" gets bold. Amazingly, the man known mostly for denouncing his Lord, for denying his relationship with Christ, for turning his eyes away from those who asked if he knew Him, wrote the following words: "But in your hearts set apart Christ as Lord. Always be prepared to give an answer to everyone who asks you to give the reason for the hope that you have. But do this with gentleness and respect, keeping a clear conscience, so that those who speak maliciously against your good behavior in Christ may be ashamed of their slander" (3:15,16). What? The guy who couldn't answer a simple question in a courtyard is now telling others "*always* be prepared to give an answer"?

Peter's proclamation reveals both his profound comprehension of forgiveness and his passionate sense of mission. He wants others to know the powerful grace of his Savior, but he has also learned that the most compelling way to introduce Him is not by pounding His truth into the heads of those listening or by presenting a neat and tidy formula for conversion. Jesus never forced Peter to believe, and He didn't present a formula either. He simply built a friendship with the fisherman.

As a result, Peter emphasized that followers of Christ should first "set [him] apart...as Lord" (3:15) and, *after* that has happened, be prepared to talk about their faith whenever someone asks. An outflow of the inflow, I like to call it. Peter was able to do both because he knew that the secret to responding with respect and gentleness came from recognizing his own sinfulness as well as God's mercy. Being forgiven by the Chief Shepherd for having failed Him in the courtyard did not make Peter superior to anyone, nor did it give him license to force others to believe as he did. It simply gave the apostle a burning desire to share the gift he'd been given with anyone who wanted to hear.

Perhaps that is also why Peter's letter included two other radical elements. For with a radical conversion came a radical lifestyle. Before his great evangelistic plea in 3:15-16, Peter completely challenged the culture of his time by spending a portion of his letter addressing women. Women at that time were second-class citizens whose identities were acknowledged and defined only through their husbands. In the context of addressing the importance of authority and submission to it—with Christ's work on the cross exhibiting the ultimate authority—Peter turned the focus to another group of people often excluded from religious discussions. In 3:1-6, the apostle radically invited women to live godly lives and to find their identities not through their husbands but through the beauty of God's favor. He also empowered them by suggesting they could actually influence men for the gospel (see 3:1). And in the same verse, which has been badly misinterpreted, Peter called women to submit to their husbands.

It is crucial, though, to recognize that Peter gave this instruction in the context of mutual submission within the whole body of Christ. First he confronted the need for governmental submission. Then he turned to economic and spiritual submission. Then he addressed the issue in a most personal and unprecedented way: with Christian wives. And he didn't stop there. He went a step further and challenged husbands to "in the same way be considerate as you live with your wives" (3:7). In other words, Peter claimed that submission is an equally important posture for every human being, regardless of social status or gender.

Where did Peter get this radical view of including and affirming those not usually included in religious circles? From watching Jesus, of course. He had seen Jesus, for example, ask a Samaritan woman for water (see John 4:1-42). He had watched Him allow a prostitute to wash His feet in front of many religious leaders, and he had seen Christ's tears when He wept openly with Mary and Martha over their brother's death (see Luke 7:36-50 and John 11:17-44). The point is not that Peter became a biblical feminist by interacting with the Prince of Peace. Rather, I think because Peter experienced the despair, shame, and injustice of his own failure, he suddenly understood what it meant to be an outcast, to be ignored and abandoned by those he considered important. Peter experienced for a short but powerful time what women lived with on a daily basis for many years. So now, like his Lord, Peter reached out to those on the fringe of society and invited them into a place of mutual respect.

Finally, it is important to remember that Peter's inclusion of women and his evangelistic plea both occurred as results of his crisis of faith. Consider the absolute humiliation Peter must have felt when he heard that rooster crow in the courtyard. Feel the pain of his demise, the shame of his decision, the sorrow he felt after failing Someone he dearly loved. Although most of us can relate to Peter, we'd rather not feel such despair. If we are honest with ourselves and one another, we don't enjoy acknowledging the utter misery of our bad choices, let alone remembering the times we've failed.

And yet Peter—the apostle, the leader, the shepherd, the rock on whom Christ's church would prevail—called Christians everywhere to "clothe yourselves with humility toward one another, because, 'God opposes the proud but gives grace to the humble'" (5:5). Peter knew that it is in humility of heart that our self-centered blinders are thrown off and we see God. It is when we acknowledge our weaknesses and imperfections that He is strong, that He is exalted as the only One who can perfect us. And it is when we yield control that we discover the freedom of real power.

Peter knew too well what happened when he did *not* humble himself under God's mighty hand. The results were devastating. So his shepherding soul cared for his flock by giving them the best practical advice any believer in Jesus needs to live a passionate yet God-pleasing life: "Humble yourselves, therefore, under God's mighty hand, that he may lift you up in due time. Cast all your anxiety on him because he cares for you" (5:6,7).

After years of learning to cast his cares on Jesus, Peter died a martyr's death. (It's believed that he was crucified upside down after enduring great persecution and exile.) Yet just as a child knows that his father will care for him, Peter reveled in his heavenly Father's care for him, and God in turn lifted him up many, many times. He had been changed, redeemed, bought with the blood of the Lamb. As a result, the Chief Shepherd used the imperfect fisherman from Galilee to influence thousands and encourage millions, to remind us that sinful, impulsive, and passionate souls have always been the instruments He uses to build His church. It is a fact whose foundation is a rock. And that's good news for those of us who want to make a difference for Christ in this present world.

MAKING IT REAL

8. What does Peter's apologetics verse teach you right now (3:15)? What difference could it make in your life?

9. How does Peter's affirmation of women affect you? In what ways could you encourage others to identify with people today who are on the fringe of society?

10. Peter spent much of his letter encouraging readers to remain humble in their love and service of one another. What are some creative ways you could apply this to your church community? (You might refer to 4:8-11 for specific ideas.)

11. Reflect for a few minutes on your life apart from Jesus. In what ways has Christ redeemed unique aspects of your personality and character as He did with Peter?

Spend some time meditating on the following verse, asking God to allow the truth of it to sink into your soul and thanking Him for the friend who wrote it in his letter to you: "And the God of all grace, who called you to his eternal glory in Christ, after you have suffered a little while, will himself restore you and make you strong, firm and steadfast. To him be the power for ever and ever. Amen" (5:10-11).

"It's hard for you, little one," said Aslan. "But things never happen the same way twice. It has been hard for us all in Narnia before now." Lucy buried her head in his mane to hide from his face. But there must have been magic in his mane. She could feel lion-strength going into her. Quite suddenly she sat up.

"I'm sorry, Aslan," she said, "I'm ready now."

"Now you are a lioness," said Aslan. "And now all Narnia will be renewed. But come. We have no time to lose."

—C. S. Lewis, *Prince Caspian,* The Chronicles of Narnia

LEADER'S NOTES

INTRODUCTION: MEETING PETER

Question for Reflection. Whenever a group of people view a movie together or read the same book, chances are good that each person will have a different perception of the story. Various elements in the tale trigger various responses, and the same can be said about people's responses to such a prominent biblical character as Peter. Allow for different perspectives as you follow the adventures of Peter. This will make for a more enriching character analysis. And remember that the point of studying his life is to learn more about the real protagonist of the Bible: Jesus Christ.

CHAPTER 1: CALLED FOR A CALLING

Question 7. One of the most interesting aspects of Christ's call to Peter is that He was not calling the fisherman to a new religion. Nor was He calling him to new religious rules, duties, or obligations. The simple pronoun "me" is a powerful reminder that Christ ultimately invited Peter—and invites us—to Himself as a Person, in an authentic life-giving relationship.

Question 10. I am a firm believer that because all humans are created in the image of a creative God, we are inherently creative beings. No one got overlooked or missed in the creativity department, though some people might not be aware of how they are creatively wired. Still, I believe each person is an artist of sorts. You might want to help one another discover some of those creative abilities, whether it's playing the piano, planting a garden, designing an engine, or cooking a meal. All reflect an essential element of living the abundant life Christ calls us to. We cannot live well or passionately without the arts, aesthetics, or creative exercises. Creativity is not a luxury; it is a necessity.

Following Jesus in a new vocation showed Peter firsthand how this was so: He heard Jesus' many parables, saw Him point out the birds of the air and the lilies as metaphors for God's provision, and probably even sang hymns with Him. As a result, Peter's own sense of creative passion was encouraged, and this probably bore much fruit in his teaching and speaking throughout the book of Acts.

CHAPTER 2: RAW PASSION

Question 2. Peter was obviously a risk taker, easily infatuated with adventures and discoveries. The fact that Jesus actually granted Peter's request to get out of the boat speaks volumes about the pleasure He derives from His children's willingness to step out. But it is important to emphasize that not every seemingly brave exploit is a wise one. Risk taking often involves very real dangers. God also gives us boundaries, limits, and healthy fears to keep us safe. In both risk taking and exercising boundaries, our steps should be taken in the light of God's presence and direction, and only when we hear Him say yes.

Question 12. Sometimes people are just as afraid to dream as they are to express their passions. Try to encourage others to assess their gifts and determine which ones will give them life rather than suck the life out of them. In other words, if people are energized by, say, painting portraits or playing the saxophone or serving others, these are most likely their God-given passions that should be developed. When we grow in our passions and offer our talents to others, the entire community of God's people is blessed and uplifted. Using our gifts is *never* only about our own fulfillment or enjoyment; it is about contributing what we can to build God's kingdom. When we hold back, everyone misses out.

CHAPTER 3: PRECOCIOUS INNOCENCE

Question 2. There are many Old Testament symbols in this encounter: They are on a mountain, two prophets known for their intimacy with God and for pointing to the coming Messiah are present, a Voice speaks through the clouds, and the humans present are not able to see God's face. Each reference here confirms the Christocentric nature of the Old Testament: All of Scripture points to Jesus, and He in turn has come to fulfill it. It might be useful to review key aspects of Moses' story (in Exodus) as well as Elijah's (in 1 and 2 Kings).

CHAPTER 4: ROCK BOTTOM

Question 1. When we read John 12:1-7, we see several parallels with the foot-washing account of John 13:1-17, specifically for Peter. In John 12, Christ allowed His feet to be washed in preparation for His death. It was a cleansing act that paved the way for Him as He prepared to die on the cross. Likewise, in John 13, Peter must allow Jesus to wash his feet because—though he did not know it—he, too, was about to die. Only his death would be a spiritual death to self, and a new self cleansed in the forgiveness of his Lord would emerge.

CHAPTER 5: BROKEN FOR GOOD

Question 7. For years there has been speculation that the 153 fish caught by the disciples represented some biblical mandate or message from God. I'd suggest not "majoring on the minors" here; rather, I believe the detail is given simply because there really were that many fish, and someone bothered to count. This detail confirms that the event really happened; it is not a piece of fiction, because in fiction such significant details would be necessary to advance the plot. This detail does not "advance" anything.

In fact, from a strictly literary perspective, the number detracts from the story. This kind of detail confirms that the story is true and reported accurately. Therefore, the reality that there were 153 fish confirms this as non-fiction rather than fiction.

Question 9. When a person crosses the line from unbelief to faith, a variety of events often produce such movement. A crisis of faith is not pleasant, yet it is exactly what God requires for us to enter into a relationship with Him. It forces us to recognize that we are more sinful and depraved than we could ever have imagined and, *at the same time,* more loved than we could ever have hoped. This is the paradox of conversion that cannot be passed over lightly, lest we develop a shallow, easy faith.

CHAPTER 6: REAL POWER

If you would like to pray for, help support, or visit the ministry Lynn runs, contact Lynn and Mark Roche, Homes of Hope, P.O. Box 17090, Suva, Fiji Islands, or e-mail them at hoh@hopefiji.org for more information.

Question 5. Every miracle we observe in Scripture is an interaction between a person and the God of the universe. Though the transforming power is offered from God, the human is allowed to receive or decline the offer. The lame man here acted in simple faith by allowing Peter to help him stand up. His spirit was willing to take the risk, but it was God who performed the healing. The Holy Spirit operated in both Peter's obedience and the man's willingness to receive God's healing.

Question 12. I want to encourage you not to rush over this beautiful description of what the early church looked like—and what it could look like today. Christians and non-Christians alike are starving to belong, to be affirmed, and to share their gifts with others. An Acts-like community of believers could be a powerful witness in today's spiritually starved culture because it moves beyond the tired rhetoric of religious talk into the active and shared life of Christian service and care.

CHAPTER 7: CONVERTED—AGAIN

Question 10. Peter's encounter with Cornelius is particularly relevant in speaking to today's tragic ethnic segregation within the church. While most Christians would never consider themselves "racists," few of us are intentional in pursuing reconciliation or in building relationships with others unlike ourselves. Yet there is an undeniably powerful witness of unity in diversity. Consider looking for creative ways that you and your church could be active in putting this critical issue on your agenda. Are there churches in your area you could partner with? Could you host international students or offer Bible studies on race relations? What would it take to develop a theology of inclusion, one that prepares you for heaven where people from all tribes and nations will gather to worship the King?

CHAPTER 8: INSPIRED TO LEAD

Question 1. Numerous examples of the issues Peter confronted in his life can be found in his letter. Consider his "new birth" (1 Peter 1:3), his constant desire to "love life and see good days" (3:10), and his understanding of the importance of the water of baptism that cleansed his sins (see 3:20-22). Each illustrates the reality that Peter personally wrestled with these issues, as we know from studying his life in the Gospels and the book of Acts. In many ways, his letter authenticates the process of spiritual growth in his life and encourages us to remember that our lives with Christ are about the daily going, not the arrival. We, like Peter, are on a journey, and we keep learning, growing, and receiving God's abundant provision of grace.

Questions 9 and 10. It might be helpful to actually write down some ways your community could respond to the needs of your neighbors, both within the church and outside it. It is always a powerful discussion to explore the specific ways you can live out your faith in Christ, how you might serve and care for the people around you in ways that clearly reflect the sacrificial and radical life of Christ. The more we get to know Jesus together, the more we cannot help but become like Him in reaching out to others who are broken and hungry for hope. And just as Peter experienced in the early church, this always happens in the context of community, with other followers of Christ.

RESOURCES FOR FURTHER THOUGHT

Baum, Lyman Frank. *The Wonderful World of Oz*. New York: Viking Penguin, 1998.

Benson, Bob and Michael W. Benson. *Disciplines for the Inner Life*. Hendersonville, Tenn.: Deeper Life, 2000.

Bruce, F. F. *New International Bible Commentary*. Grand Rapids: Zondervan, 1999.

Collodi, Carlo. *Pinocchio*. London: Puffin Books, 1996.

Day, Dorothy. "By Little and by Little." In *Dorothy Day: Selected Writings*. Edited by Robert Ellsberg. New York: Orbis, 1983.

Grant, Michael. *Saint Peter: A Biography*. New York: Simon & Schuster, 1995.

Guroian, Vigen. *Tending the Heart of Virtue: How Classic Stories Awaken a Child's Moral Imagination*. New York: Oxford University Press, 2002.

King, Martin Luther, Jr. *The Strength to Love*. In *A Testament of Hope: The Essential Writings and Speeches of Martin Luther King, Jr.* Edited by James M. Washington. San Francisco: HarperSan-Francisco, 2003.

Lewis, C. S. *Prince Caspian*. New York: HarperCollins, 2002.

———. *The Horse and His Boy*. New York: HarperCollins, 2002.

———. *The Silver Chair*. New York: HarperCollins, 2002.

Milne, A. A. *Winnie the Pooh*. New York: Penguin Putnam, Dutton/Plume, 1999.

Newbigin, Lesslie. *The Light Has Come: An Exposition of the Fourth Gospel*. Grand Rapids: Eerdmans, 1987.

Nouwen, Henri J. M., Donald M. McNeill, and Douglas A. Morrison. *Compassion: A Reflection on the Christian Life.* New York: Doubleday, 1983.

Perkins, Pheme. *Peter: Apostle for the Whole Church.* Minneapolis: Augsburg, 2000.

Wangerin, Walter, Jr. *The Book of the Dun Cow.* San Francisco: HarperSanFrancisco, 1989.

White, E. B. *Charlotte's Web.* New York: HarperCollins, 2002.

Williams, Margery. *The Velveteen Rabbit.* New York: HarperCollins, Morrow/Avon, 1999.

FOR FURTHER STUDY

If you enjoyed this Fisherman Resource, you might want to explore our full line of Fisherman Resources and Bible Studyguides. The following books offer time-tested Fisherman inductive Bible studies for individuals or groups.

FISHERMAN RESOURCES

The Art of Spiritual Listening: Responding to God's Voice Amid the Noise of Life by Alice Fryling

Balm in Gilead by Dudley Delffs

The Essential Bible Guide by Whitney T. Kuniholm

Questions from the God Who Needs No Answers: What Is He Really Asking of You? by Carolyn and Craig Williford

Reckless Faith: Living Passionately as Imperfect Christians by Jo Kadlecek

Soul Strength: Spiritual Courage for the Battles of Life by Pam Lau

FISHERMAN BIBLE STUDYGUIDES

Topical Studies

Angels by Vinita Hampton Wright

Becoming Women of Purpose by Ruth Haley Barton

Building Your House on the Lord: A Firm Foundation for Family Life (Revised Edition) by Steve and Dee Brestin

Discipleship: The Growing Christian's Lifestyle by James and Martha Reapsome

Doing Justice, Showing Mercy: Christian Action in Today's World by Vinita Hampton Wright

Encouraging Others: Biblical Models for Caring by Lin Johnson

The End Times: Discovering What the Bible Says by E. Michael Rusten

Examining the Claims of Jesus by Dee Brestin

Friendship: Portraits in God's Family Album by Steve and Dee Brestin

The Fruit of the Spirit: Growing in Christian Character by Stuart Briscoe

Great Doctrines of the Bible by Stephen Board

Great Passages of the Bible by Carol Plueddemann

Great Prayers of the Bible by Carol Plueddemann

Growing Through Life's Challenges by James and Martha Reapsome

Guidance & God's Will by Tom and Joan Stark

Heart Renewal: Finding Spiritual Refreshment by Ruth Goring

Higher Ground: Steps Toward Christian Maturity by Steve and Dee Brestin

Images of Redemption: God's Unfolding Plan Through the Bible by Ruth E. Van Reken

Integrity: Character from the Inside Out by Ted W. Engstrom and Robert C. Larson

Lifestyle Priorities by John White

Marriage: Learning from Couples in Scripture by R. Paul and Gail Stevens

Miracles by Robbie Castleman

One Body, One Spirit: Building Relationships in the Church by Dale and Sandy Larsen

The Parables of Jesus by Gladys Hunt

Parenting with Purpose and Grace by Alice Fryling

Prayer: Discovering What Scripture Says by Timothy Jones and Jill Zook-Jones

The Prophets: God's Truth Tellers by Vinita Hampton Wright

Proverbs and Parables: God's Wisdom for Living by Dee Brestin

Satisfying Work: Christian Living from Nine to Five by R. Paul Stevens and Gerry Schoberg

Senior Saints: Growing Older in God's Family by James and Martha
    Reapsome
The Sermon on the Mount: The God Who Understands Me by Gladys
    M. Hunt
Speaking Wisely: Exploring the Power of Words by Poppy Smith
Spiritual Disciplines: The Tasks of a Joyful Life by Larry Sibley
Spiritual Gifts by Karen Dockrey
Spiritual Hunger: Filling Your Deepest Longings by Jim and Carol
    Plueddemann
A Spiritual Legacy: Faith for the Next Generation by Chuck and Winnie
    Christensen
Spiritual Warfare by A. Scott Moreau
The Ten Commandments: God's Rules for Living by Stuart Briscoe
Ultimate Hope for Changing Times by Dale and Sandy Larsen
When Faith Is All You Have: A Study of Hebrews 11 by Ruth
    E. Van Reken
Where Your Treasure Is: What the Bible Says About Money by James and
    Martha Reapsome
Who Is God? by David P. Seemuth
Who Is Jesus? In His Own Words by Ruth E. Van Reken
Who Is the Holy Spirit? by Barbara H. Knuckles and Ruth E. Van Reken
Wisdom for Today's Woman: Insights from Esther by Poppy Smith
Witnesses to All the World: God's Heart for the Nations by Jim and Carol
    Plueddemann
Women at Midlife: Embracing the Challenges by Jeanie Miley
Worship: Discovering What Scripture Says by Larry Sibley

Bible Book Studies
Genesis: Walking with God by Margaret Fromer and Sharrel Keyes
Exodus: God Our Deliverer by Dale and Sandy Larsen

Ruth: Relationships That Bring Life by Ruth Haley Barton

Ezra and Nehemiah: A Time to Rebuild by James Reapsome

(For Esther, see Topical Studies, *Wisdom for Today's Woman*)

Job: Trusting Through Trials by Ron Klug

Psalms: A Guide to Prayer and Praise by Ron Klug

Proverbs: Wisdom That Works by Vinita Hampton Wright

Ecclesiastes: A Time for Everything by Stephen Board

Song of Songs: A Dialogue of Intimacy by James Reapsome

Jeremiah: The Man and His Message by James Reapsome

Jonah, Habakkuk, and Malachi: Living Responsibly by Margaret Fromer
      and Sharrel Keyes

Matthew: People of the Kingdom by Larry Sibley

Mark: God in Action by Chuck and Winnie Christensen

Luke: Following Jesus by Sharrel Keyes

John: The Living Word by Whitney Kuniholm

Acts 1–12: God Moves in the Early Church by Chuck and Winnie
      Christensen

Acts 13–28, see *Paul* under Character Studies

Romans: The Christian Story by James Reapsome

1 Corinthians: Problems and Solutions in a Growing Church by Charles
      and Ann Hummel

Strengthened to Serve: 2 Corinthians by Jim and Carol Plueddemann

Galatians, Titus, and Philemon: Freedom in Christ by Whitney Kuniholm

Ephesians: Living in God's Household by Robert Baylis

Philippians: God's Guide to Joy by Ron Klug

Colossians: Focus on Christ by Luci Shaw

Letters to the Thessalonians by Margaret Fromer and Sharrel Keyes

Letters to Timothy: Discipleship in Action by Margaret Fromer and Sharrel
      Keyes

Hebrews: Foundations for Faith by Gladys Hunt

James: Faith in Action by Chuck and Winnie Christensen

1 and 2 Peter, Jude: Called for a Purpose by Steve and Dee Brestin
1, 2, 3 John: How Should a Christian Live? by Dee Brestin
Revelation: The Lamb Who Is the Lion by Gladys Hunt

Bible Character Studies
Abraham: Model of Faith by James Reapsome
David: Man After God's Own Heart by Robbie Castleman
Elijah: Obedience in a Threatening World by Robbie Castleman
Great People of the Bible by Carol Plueddemann
King David: Trusting God for a Lifetime by Robbie Castleman
Men Like Us: Ordinary Men, Extraordinary God by Paul Heidebrecht
          and Ted Scheuermann
Moses: Encountering God by Greg Asimakoupoulos
Paul: Thirteenth Apostle (Acts 13–28) by Chuck and Winnie Christensen
Women Like Us: Wisdom for Today's Issues by Ruth Haley Barton
Women Who Achieved for God by Winnie Christensen
Women Who Believed God by Winnie Christensen

ABOUT THE AUTHOR

JO KADLECEK has been teaching Bible studies, Sunday-school classes, re-treats, and academic college courses for the past fifteen years. She has been an active member of Redeemer Presbyterian Church in New York City since 1996 and an urban neighbor for the past sixteen years. She holds master's degrees in communication and humanities.

AN INNOVATIVE, PRACTICAL APPROACH TO BIBLE STUDY

FISHERMAN RESOURCES

Fisherman Resources offer a unique blend of traditional, inductive Bible study and imaginative elements focusing on spiritual renewal and intimacy with God. These guides maintain the integrity of Fisherman inductive studies while adding more text, more stories, and more creative activities and questions. Inside you'll find such inventive additions as multimedia bibliographies and guidelines for spiritual retreats, along with exercises in Bible study, prayer, and self-reflection—all designed to help you direct your attention to what God is doing in your life.

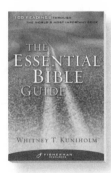

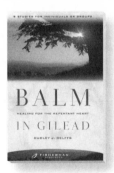

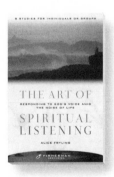

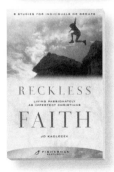

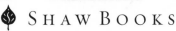

SHAW BOOKS

www.shawbooks.com